## Lunch Menu

### Aperitifs

Pastis Tasting $12

Shinriku "Sacred Power" Sake $4

Hidalgo Manzanilla Sherry "La Gitana" $5

Lustau Dry Fino Sherry $6

Ferrand Pineau di Charentes $7

Lillet $6

Herbsaint Cocktail $5.5

Campari and Soda $5.5

### Sparkling Wines

Nino Franco

Prosecco Rive 2000 $7

Pierre Peters

Brut Champagne N/V $13

### Cocktails

Absente Traditional $6

Billie Holiday $8

The Streetcar $6

Haitian Daiquiri $7

Half Sinner Half Saint $6

Traditional Sazerac $7

Kurant Cosmopolitan $7

Caipirinha $6.5

Citadelle Greyhound $6

Pimms Cup $6

### White Wine Flight $12
### Alsace

Bott Pinot Gris

Paul Blanck Riesling "Classic"

Weinbach Riesling "Cuvee Theo"

### Red Wine Flight $12
### Pinot Noir

Gagnoux Bourgogne Rouge

Casa Carneros '97

Girardin Savigny les Beaunes "Lavieres"

### SOUPS AND SALADS

Herbsaint, Tomato and Shrimp Bisque $6

Gumbo of the Day $6

Mixed Greens with Dried Figs, Walnuts, Great Hill Blue Cheese and Sherry Vinaigrette $6

Hearts of Romaine with Roasted Garlic Dressing and Anchovies $6

Shrimp Stuffed Deviled Eggs with Baby Spinach and Bacon Vinaigrette $8

Arugula and Endive with Rabbit Croquettes and Whole Grain Mustard Vinaigrette $9

### SMALL PLATES

Antipasto Plate-
  Marinated Eggplant and Shiitake Mushrooms,
  Chicken Terrine, Salami and Sheeps Milk Cheese $11

Cornmeal-Fried Oysters with Cole Slaw and Hot Sauce $8

Shrimp and Green Chile Grits Cakes with Tasso Cream Sauce $10

Fried Frog Legs with Fresh Fines Herbs $9

Herb Gnocchi with Wild Mushrooms, Sage and Roasted Garlic $9

### MAIN COURSES

Chicken, Italian Sausage Ballotine and Pappardelle with Mushrooms and Sage Madeira Jus $14

Grilled Salmon Sandwich with Arugula and Lemon Pickle Mayonnaise with Yukon Gold Chips $10

Tuscan Style White Bean Stew with Butternut Squash and Greens $12

Herbsaint Hamburger with Grilled Onions and Farmhouse Cheddar $10

Yellowfin Tuna Salad with Grilled Fennel, Arugula, and Lemon Garlic Vinaigrette $12

Pan Roasted Gulf Shrimp with Romesco and Toasted Almonds $14

Fish of the Day   Market

### SIDES $4

Coleslaw                              Green Vegetable of the Day

French Fries with Pimenton Aioli      Marinated Eggplant

An eighteen percent gratuity will be added to parties of 7 or more.

A $3 Valet Parking charge will be added to your check when applicable.

Smoking is permitted in the bar only.

---

## Dinner Menu

D0118747

...ke $4

...o Gitana" $5

Sherry Vinaigrette $6

...ottes and Whole Grain Mustard Vinaigrette $9

### SMALL PLATES

Antipasto Plate with Marinated Eggplant and Shiitake Mushrooms,
Duck Terrine, House Cured Meat and Sheeps Milk Cheese $11

Shrimp and Green Chile Grits Cakes with Tasso Cream Sauce $10

Fried Frog Legs with Fresh Fines Herbs $9

Herb Gnocchi with Wild Mushrooms, Sage and Roasted Garlic $9

Beef Short Rib on Potato Cake with Dijon-Horseradish Dressing $12

### ...IN COURSES

...arian Special $14

...the Day   Market Price

...d Pepper Roasted Shrimp with Creamy Polenta and Shellfish Broth $22

...icasee with Homemade Pappardelle and Wild Mushrooms $19

...ed Free Range Chicken with Wild Mushroom and Bacon Hash $19

...d Kurobuta Pork Belly with Beluga Lentils and Mint $19

...ck Leg Confit with Dirty Rice and Citrus Gastrique $20

...of the Day $4

...Pimenton Aioli $4          Marinated Eggplant $4

                             Dirty Rice  $5

...will be added to parties of 7 or more.

...be added to your check when applicable.

...only.

creole nouvelle

# CONTEMPORARY
# CREOLE
## COOKERY

*Joseph Carey*

**TAYLOR TRADE**
Lanham • New York • Dallas • Boulder • Toronto • Oxford

Published by Taylor Trade Publishing
An imprint of The Rowman & Littlefield Publishing Group, Inc.
4501 Forbes Boulevard, Suite 200
Lanham, Maryland 20706

Distributed by National Book Network

Library of Congress Cataloging-in-Publication Data

Carey, Joseph, 1942-
  Creole nouvelle : contemporary creole cookery / Joseph
Carey.— 1st Taylor Trade pub. ed.
      p. cm.
  Includes index.
  ISBN 1-58979-130-4 (cloth : alk. paper)
  1. Cookery, American—Louisiana style. 2. Cookery, Cajun.
3. Cookery, Creole. I. Title.
  TX715.2.L68C36 2004
  641.59763—dc22          2004005884

♾ ™ The paper used in this publication meets the minimum requirements of
American National Standard for Information Sciences—Permanence of
Paper for Printed Library Materials, ANSI/NISO Z39.48—1992.
Manufactured in the United States of America.

# ❧ DEDICATION ❧

For my first typist, Lovey Cornelia, my mother.
I hope she has found that peace which passeth understanding.

# contents

# ACKNOWLEDGMENTS

Of course, it would be impossible to thank all the people who got me to the point where I could write this book.

Anne Kearney, Susan Spicer, Donald Link, John Harris, and Peter Vazquez were all very kind and helpful contributors. Without the hard work, talent, and vision of these chefs, there would have been no Creole Nouvelle cuisine and no book. As I honed the final version of *Creole Nouvelle*, Anne's husband, Tom; Peter's wife, Janis; and Susan's assistant, Ginger, all helped me with the fine points.

My mother, Lovey Cornelia; father, Joseph; and Aunt Maye are all gone. I don't know that I ever told my mother how much I liked her Red Beans and Rice. My Aunt Maye presided at the awakening of my taste buds. And my daddy introduced me to the world.

My agent, Peter Rubie, hung in there with me, and my editor, Camille Cline, who I sometimes cursed and often grumbled to, marked up just about every page I ever sent her. She made it a better book.

Deirdre Stanforth's *New Orleans Restaurant Cookbook* (1967) and *The Picayune Creole Cookbook* (1901) were my principal memory aids.

I bounced the original concept off Ann Rule. She liked it and encouraged me to continue with it.

And, of course, my old running buddy, Denis Kelly, writer, teacher, and bon vivant, read the book and was kind enough to write a foreword.

Many of these recipes for the serious home cook were developed in my evening classes. Without the assistance of my many volunteer helpers, I could not have taught these classes. Beverly, Wyman, Ralph, John, and John—thank you.

Last, and most certainly not least, I would like to thank all the students, both professional and serious amateur, who have studied with me and asked the questions that made me want to keep learning.

# ABOUT THE TITLE

The name *Creole Nouvelle* is my term for the kind of cooking I see going on in the best restaurants in New Orleans today. Some of the chefs who have kindly contributed recipes to me for this book will quibble with the term. The original Creole cookery—we'll call it *Vieux Creole* to distinguish it from *Creole Nouvelle*—was *principally* French with some Spanish, maybe a little Italian, and local Louisiana influences. The best of the genre was to be found in restaurants owned or run by creative, professionally trained chefs who observed classical techniques, were most emphatically *not* cooking *in* France or Spain or Italy, and used only the freshest ingredients with an eye to appearance and taste, as well as nutrition. Unfortunately, what we have termed "Creole" cuisine over the years has become kind of tired and banal. It has lost its innovative, eclectic verve. Repetition and imitation to curry favor with the tourist dollar was the whoop du jour. That era has come to an end, folks.

Some of the chefs in the book object to the term because of the common association of the term "Creole" in the public mind (particularly out-of-town diners) with restaurants, many of them well known, that serve gumbos, jambalaya, shrimp Creole, po' boys and the southern Louisiana hodgepodge of both Creole and Cajun. Not that there is anything wrong with any of those dishes when well made. Quite the contrary. You are unlikely to find many of these dishes at any of the restaurants that contributed to this book. If you do, the version will be vastly different from the traditional versions; an excellent example is Anne Kearney's Oysters "Rockefeller" (see page 53), a dish of poached—not baked—oysters with a classic velouté or Cuvée's Crisp Mirliton and Spicy Shrimp Rémoulade Napoleon. While I have had enjoyable meals at Cuvée, it missed the final cut for the book because the owner is not in the kitchen, as is the case with all the other restaurants in the book.

There is a fairly short list of older Creole restaurants in New Orleans today. Some are gone forever—Corinne Dunbar's and Masson's come to mind. The oldest Creole restaurant, Antoine's (1840), is still going strong. I have my versions of recipes for several of their dishes I remember from my youth here in the book: Oysters Rockefeller, Eggs Sardou, and Baked Alaska are stalwarts there. My culinary Virgil was my Aunt Maye, who guided me through the gastronomic byways of a city that just effuses restaurants. We went to places she liked and where she was known. Galatoire's was probably her favorite, and we ate there most often, although Delmonico's was a close second. With the exception of the latter, do not look for anything new or innovative on any of these menus. The only thing new in Galatoire's is the facelift the restaurant got in 1999.

I did not know the chefs in those days. In that era, there were few celebrity chefs. The restaurant was all. The restaurant owners set the tone then. They were the stars. Arnaud Cazenave—quite possibly the reluctant inventor of the Mimosa—of Arnaud's and Madame Begué—although she was before my time—of what became Tujague's were two of the better-known New Orleans' characters. She is credited with inventing the meal we now call "brunch." My godfather was the maître d' at The Blue Room in the Hotel Roosevelt—now the New Orleans Fairmont Hotel. While the Sazerac Bar in the hotel may not have invented the absinthe drink of the same name, they were certainly the most noted purveyor of it. The representative of this old guard of Creole restaurants in which I have eaten most often recently is Commander's Palace. Although the cuisine changes with the chef—and they do change chefs, though I would not be comfortable citing the name of one here and now—one can always count on world-class service there if not new dishes.

It is a new day. Whatever term the chefs themselves choose to describe their cuisine, I think these five chefs—Anne Kearney of Peristyle, Susan Spicer of Bayona, John Harris of Lilette, Donald Link of Herbsaint, and Peter Vazquez of Marisol—represent the very best of contemporary New Orleans cookery—a cuisine that can stand up tall to *anything* being done in New York, Los Angeles, or Chicago.

You must plan ahead to eat in the restaurants mentioned in *Creole Nouvelle*. Do not count on blowing into town and getting a last-minute reservation. Tom Sand, Anne Kearney's husband and co-proprietor of Peristyle, told me what he says to tourists who have not planned ahead and who just must eat at Peristyle. "It's just food," he tells them with a wry grin. It may be "just food," but if you miss sampling the food at these restaurants while in New Orleans, you will be kicking yourself later.

In the year it took to complete this book there have been some changes to the New Orleans dining scene. Anne Kearney and her husband Tom Sand have sold Peristyle to Tom Wolfe, another well-known New Orleans chef. They could have sold the restaurant to many interested parties, but Anne had worked with and trusts Tom Wolfe. There will be few changes to the menu and the sous chef in the kitchen actually remains the same.

# ❧ FOREWORD ☙

## *Creole Nouvelle* and Chef Joseph Carey

## Denis Kelly

When I heard that Chef Joseph Carey was writing a book about a creative new style of cooking in New Orleans and environs, *Creole Nouvelle*, I thought, "There's a match made in culinary heaven!" I've known Joe Carey since our college days, when we both discovered our lifelong passions for making and eating great food. I cooked and worked with him during the San Francisco Bay Area Food Renaissance at restaurants, at parties, and for many wine and food events. And over the years, some of the finest dishes I've ever eaten have been Chef Carey's creations. He has a deep commitment to quality and the finest ingredients and a keen sensory intelligence that brings out the core of flavor, the essence of taste, in any dish or recipe he puts his hand to.

What has always impressed me about Joe Carey's cooking is his ability to use classical techniques to re-create traditional recipes with a creative flair that lets you taste food in a new and exciting way. His grounding in the classic Creole dishes of his native New Orleans and his training in the methods of French cuisine merge with this spirit of creativity in a new style of cooking. He approaches the cooking of New Orleans with an original perspective gained from his experiences in California, in Asia, and at some of the finest restaurants in the South. *Creole Nouvelle* draws on his own experiences and the work of a new generation of chefs in New Orleans who have revitalized the city's great cuisine.

Creole cooking, the lively and eclectic cuisine of New Orleans, melds together flavors from a wealth of food traditions from France, Spain, Africa, and Native American cultures. Cajun cookery, its country cousin, has gained more note of late, but both styles of regional Louisiana cooking have given us some of the great classics of American cuisine. James Beard, the paterfamilias of American regional cooking, inscribed his book *American Cookery* to me with the words, "Yes Denis, there is an American cuisine!" And the cooking of New Orleans and southern Louisiana is one of the foundations of our American cookery.

But as with all traditions, the classics can sometimes grow stale, become clichés, and turn into commercialized, pale versions of the original. Too often, the great dishes degenerate into standard versions turned out by mass-market restaurants and food processors—bland pasta Alfredo and soft, spongy pizzas; haute cuisine continentale with one sauce fits all; blackened something or other and soggy jambalaya.

What Joe Carey has done in *Creole Nouvelle* is to (literally) re-create the great classics of New Orleans by working with young chefs who are at the forefront of a renaissance in Louisiana cookery. Like the creators of nouvelle cuisine in France who enlivened and brightened the faded flavors of classic haute cuisine, these creative chefs have brought new energy and imagination to this great tradition. Chef Carey presents their reworking of traditional dishes and their creation of new combinations of traditional ingredients in his book. He also contributes innovative and delicious recipes of his own that merge his native New Orleans roots with his classical training and exposure to many culinary traditions through his time in California, Europe, and Asia. An example of this creative fusion is Carey's Tea-Smoked Duck Gumbo Filé with Poached Oysters, a tasty amalgam of a traditional Creole gumbo filé and the Chinese delicacy, tea-smoked duck.

I can't wait to cook (and eat) dishes like Cream of Garlic Soup and Crab and Coconut Soup, Boudin-Stuffed Quail with Fig Sauce, and Braised Duck on Buttermilk Biscuit with Blood Orange Marmalade. Maybe I'll round out the meal with an old favorite that I remember Joe always ended our Creole feasts with: Raisin and Brandy Bread Pudding. This is a book for anyone who loves to cook and eat the classic dishes of Creole cookery, a great cuisine reinterpreted and enlivened by a new generation of New Orleans chefs.

Denis Kelly is author of *Grilling & Barbecuing: Food & Fire in American Regional Cooking* and *Essentials of Grilling* and coauthor of *The Complete Meat Cookbook.*

# ∾ INTRODUCTION ∾

The palpable, vagrant, even insolent smells, sights, and sounds of the Vieux Carré (French Quarter) in New Orleans have seduced residents and visitors alike for over 300 years now. While the black Creole women of New Orleans no longer sashay the steamy early morning streets of the French Quarter calling, "Belle Cala. Tout Chaud," selling their Creole Rice Cakes (calas) to be eaten with the morning coffee (they were still doing this when *The Picayune Creole Cookbook* came out in 1901), there is no shortage of traditional aromas, sights, and first-light cacophony in today's Vieux Carré. Produce is bickered over in the market. Shutters on Creole cottages and storefronts slam open, and sidewalks are hosed as restaurants and saloons prepare for another day. There is no city in the New World like New Orleans. The Morning Call has moved to Metairie (worth the trip), but Café du Monde has taken its place, providing the still, expectant mornings in the Quarter with the sweet fragrance of fried fritters splashed with powdered sugar—beignets—and strong Creole coffee.

Just up the street at the Central Grocery, the cooks are making the olive dressing for their famous Muffuletta. Some things have changed, but like the river, New Orleans, the Quarter, and Creole food just keep on rollin' along. Between the Café du Monde and the Central Grocery, on Decatur, the bar at Tujague's is already open. This was where my daddy took me to eat most often. Every Monday, my mother, just like every other mother in New Orleans, made Haricot Rouge et Riz (Red Beans and Rice), and at least once a week my daddy picked up Stuffed Artichokes or Barbecued Shrimp at Manales on Napoleon. Another tradition, the Friday lunch, is still observed—even in those restaurants that do not serve lunch Monday through Thursday.

The French Quarter's street boundaries are clearly delineated. It consists of *about* 120 blocks, depending on which way you count. The Quarter itself is oriented more or less southwest to northeast, although you will hear "north, south, east, and west." On the southwest, the street boundaries are Iberville and Canal; on the northwest, Basin and Rampart Streets; on the northeast, Esplanade; and on the southeast, Decatur (although the Quarter actually extends beyond Decatur, to the river, there are no more *named* streets past it). Toward the northeast is a quieter, more residential—although it is getting noisier—section of the Quarter called the Lower Quarter.

Two of the restaurants I mention here, Peristyle and Bayona, are actually in the French Quarter, but one is only marginally out of it (Marisol is on the Marigny side of Esplanade), and the other two may be easily reached by orienting oneself from the Quarter. Lilette is on Magazine; one of the streets in the Quarter, Decatur, becomes Magazine after one crosses Canal. Royal, one of the main streets in the Quarter, becomes St. Charles across Canal, and there is where we'll find Herbsaint. The face of the entire city is still permeated with the centuries of French and Spanish cultural saturation like no other city in the Americas. Appropriately, several of the chefs here in this book have spent time in France or worked under chefs who did, and one is of Latin extraction.

In this book, I present many of the classic New Orleans Creole recipes in new and improved (in that the recipes follow classical principles and are quicker, lighter, and healthier) format, along with a few new recipes of my own. Many of the Creole cookbooks I have seen over the years do not follow classical techniques, and the results tend to be hit or miss. I'll also feature several recipes from the chefs in New Orleans who are leading the way with this newer Creole cookery. I think this culinary movement features the densest concentration of creative and innovative chefs in the country at this time. Much attention has been paid to Cajun-style cooking in the past few years, with but little notice being taken of New Orlean's unique, indigenous style of cookery—*Creole*.

When I am not teaching, I spend my time in New Orleans. I make a point to keep in touch with its chefs and food writers, and I try to eat in every quality restaurant there as often as time affords. I speak with chefs, managers, and owners and do my best to keep my finger on the pulse of the New Orleans restaurant scene. My location away from the city, but with ready access to its charms, gives me a perspective on the Creole cuisine I would not have if I were involved in the day-to-day hustle for the food dollar in New Orleans.

## CREOLE AND CAJUN

What is the difference between *Cajun* and *Creole*? While never jejune, the diet of the typical Creole may have never been quite as hearty as that of the Cajun. I have to admit the lines between the two cuisines have become somewhat blurred over the years with the growth in New Orleans restaurants and the popularity of Cajun cooking thanks, principally, to Chef Paul Prudhomme. I'll attempt to illustrate what I believe are the main differences here in a few paragraphs.

The two styles of cookery began very differently. For centuries, New Orleans has been a cooking pot of nationalities—Spanish, Italian, Portuguese, French, African, Native American, German, and, yes, even Irish, says Chef Carey, and a few cultures I'm sure I'm leaving out inadvertently. Each has contributed its special ingredients and styles of food, seasoning, and preparation to the food that I am calling "Creole."

Creole cooking is a more sophisticated, more urban, more classical style, while Cajun, a country style, relies more on rustic ingredients. Creole was more influenced by the classical cookery of Europe and Cajun more by the ingredients naturally available to those used to "living off the land." The Cajuns have often had to "make do" with what they had. The Creoles of New Orleans would send their cooks or chefs to the market to buy ingredients for Old World recipes. Many of these ingredients in the original dishes were not available, and often the cooks would substitute to the best of their abilities with whatever local ingredients they could find in the market, much as Anne Kearney and like-minded chefs do today. You might say that the Creole cookery of New Orleans developed on its own, organically, as a result of the clash and confluence of many separate cultures.

Cajun cookery, on the other hand, is a result of the intermingling of the Cajuns with the folks already residing in southern Louisiana. The British expelled the Cajuns (the word *Cajun* is a corruption of *Acadian*, which itself is a corruption of *Arcadian*) from Acadia in Nova Scotia in 1755; this expulsion is known as "Le Grand Derangement." They became a kind of latter-day Gallic Diaspora, with families and lovers torn from each other and scattered to destinations as far away as the West Indies, Georgia, and the Falkland Islands. (Longfellow's poem *Evangeline*, with much poetic license, details the story of Evangeline and Gabriel and the sojourn of the Acadians to Louisiana.) Choctaws and Houmas introduced local ingredients to those landing in southwestern Louisiana ("Acadiana"). The new immigrants also mixed with local Germans who arrived in Louisiana around 1690 and brought their sausage-making skills to Louisiana with them. I suppose we *could* describe Cajun cuisine as "down home" New World French.

## WHY THIS COOKBOOK?

This book is a paean to traditional Creole food and a reworking of some of the classic dishes as well as a harbinger of the new era in Creole cookery. My dishes will be more basic as well as simpler and easier (for the most part) to execute than some of the chefs' contributions. I feature dishes I have created and some I have reworked along with many recipes from some of New Orleans's most talented chefs who have their own new slants on, and creative notions of, what *I* call Creole cuisine. I have not tampered at all with any of the other chefs' recipes, except to reorganize them into a more accessible format.

Over the years, as I have been away from New Orleans learning, working, traveling, and teaching—Europe, Asia, New York, California, Chicago, and Memphis—I have found myself changing the ways in which I prepared traditional Creole dishes. In my many forays back to my hometown, I have paid careful attention to the new chefs and what they were up to. I noticed that many of them were reaching conclusions quite similar to mine. Subtly and unconsciously at first, I learned more and more of classical European technique and a smattering of Oriental techniques and the reasons for them.

The cooking we were doing in California during the 1970s and 1980s in the San Francisco Bay Area Food Renaissance is not at all different from that done traditionally by classical chefs the world over—an emphasis on fresh, local, in-season ingredients handled with care. As time went on and I taught more and more, more consciously, with various ends in mind—sometimes flavor, sometimes texture, sometimes nutrition—I asked myself why I did this or that, what was the benefit to this ingredient or that procedure. I found my students asking me the same questions I was asking myself. I began to take stock. I examined all my recipes and why I did what with each. I made some startling discoveries. In some recipes, I had violated everything I knew about classical technique. When I corrected these "violations," the dishes invariably improved. I have attempted to eliminate *all* wasted moves from my cooking and the techniques I teach. I tell my students that if a chef cannot instantly tell you why he or she does any given thing, be wary. Much useless, wasteful lore is passed from generation to generation.

Although I had been cooking Creole cuisine in the Bay Area since 1971, the above revelations did not come to me all at once. The process was aided by my trips to New Orleans. As I have visited my birthplace over the past several years, I have run across several chefs who have independently decided to "modernize" and "professionalize" Creole cookery. By that I mean the younger chefs (and some not so young) who have been classically trained or have served fruitful apprenticeships and are bringing sound culinary technique to this new cooking. No wasted moves.

Several of the newer restaurants in which I have eaten are doing very impressive work with ingredients available today in southern Louisiana. I will be including recipes and menus from some of these chefs—Susan Spicer of Bayona, Anne Kearney of Peristyle, John Harris of Lilette, Donald Link of Herbsaint, and Peter Vazquez of Marisol. Most of these folks were not reared in New Orleans. As I was on the train out of town, they were on their way in. They have entrenched themselves, have adopted and been adopted by the city, and are invigorating the cuisine. A player in this movement is the peripatetic Crescent City Market (not to be confused with the French Market). I'll tell you a little about that right before we get to the restaurants.

While these are certainly not the *only* places to eat in New Orleans, they are all places you will *want* to eat. You will need to call ahead. These restaurants have been featured in national food magazines, and the chefs have won numerous awards. I have now come back to the first food I was exposed to with a renewed interest and vigor. My time away has given me a perspective I do not think I would have had otherwise. I do think that some of the best food in the world is to be had in New Orleans.

I feel great solidarity with the chefs featured in this book. There is a fraternity among chefs. It has nothing to do with any sanctioning organization. It has to do with attitude. Chefs who are "real" recognize this reality in others instantly. While there is no single characteristic shared by all, here are some of the things they are likely to have in common: curiosity, intelligence, a sense of adventure, an impeccable work ethic, and an insistence on the very best raw materials at hand. Their eyes, palates, and culinary integrity produce memorable dining experiences. I am afraid that this country is more and more rife with "bag 'em, gag 'em, and tag 'em" establishments that do not care about the quality of the dining experience nearly as much as they care about the bottom line. I am proud to say that the current proliferation of quality dining establishments in New Orleans is running contrary to this trend.

The chefs featured here have been kind enough to share a few of their recipes and thoughts with me. I am sure that all of them will be out with their own distinctive cookbooks in due time. Here I am just trying to give you a feel for the new energy and excitement that has been infused in a classic, distinctive, regional American cookery in my favorite city.

Many of my recipes were developed during the years I spent in the San Francisco Bay Area as a chef. Chef Donald Link of Herbsaint was also cooking contemporary Creole cuisine in the Bay Area a little after my time there. While I did not have access to some of the ingredients characteristic of classic Creole cookery, I did have access to a wonderful array of fresh fruits and vegetables, seafoods, and artisanal cheeses; we were using Laura Chenel's goat cheese very early on. Her cheeses have now spread all over the country, and newer cheese artisans, such as the Cowgirl Creamery, are making their presence known—although, there *was* a wonderful market in downtown Oakland called The Housewife's Market. Very much like a European marketplace or one of the *old* New Orleans markets, the market featured individual stalls from small vendors with a particular Louisiana cast. This was all under one roof in a large warehouse. I bought locally made boudin blanc and andouille there as well as live Gulf blue crabs. I bought fresh okra for gumbo here. I once bought two kids (no, not that kind!) from a vendor here for a wine dinner. A few short blocks away was the Oakland wholesale produce market, where I purchased fresh produce for years. Jack London Square separates these two areas.

## TECHNIQUES IN THE KITCHEN

Each of the classical techniques we will bring to the Creole preparations has long and venerable roots reaching far back into the history of cookery. In the first chapter, we will examine them and a few of the ingredients in Creole cookery. Once you know these techniques and are familiar with some of the ingredients, you will find your enjoyment in the kitchen increase immensely.

The dishes may seem somewhat eclectic to you. They are. The New Orleans Creole culture is among the most diverse. Throughout the book, you will note dishes that appear to be Italian or French or "soul food"; each has its own unique Creole interpretation. The cooking of the Creoles may remind you of the cooking of the Mediterranean. This is not coincidence. Many of the French, Italians, and Spanish who developed this cookery were from the Mediterranean areas of those respective countries. Many of the same ingredients, or ones very like those of the European Mediterranean, grow and thrive in the climate of southern Louisiana. These dishes are characterized by a liberal use of olive oil, tomatoes, onions, garlic, bell and other peppers, and dishes with multilayered spicing. By that, I do not mean "hot." Creole food is not necessarily hot—spicy hot, I mean.

The Creole cuisine is constantly evolving—and has been for nearly 300 years—but the current evolution is more of a revolution. Changes are occurring quickly and innovatively. This revolution is driven by mostly young (and as I age, so does my notion of what "young" is) chefs who are bringing classical technique and new notions of freshness of ingredients along with clever combinations of those fresh ingredients. I try to make the techniques crystal clear in each of the recipes in *Creole Nouvelle*. This is the kind of thing the serious home cook is looking for and has asked me for in my classes. I teach evening classes to the serious home cook, and the one class that is always the biggest is the New Orleans class. Creole cuisine is fare that many of these folks think they know—until I get my hands on them and on it. I stress technique and provide them with a new approach to cooking. I usually teach this class three or four times per year, and it is not at all unusual to see the same faces taking the class more than once.

Finally, remember that I am not a restaurant critic. I am a chef. A restaurant critic walks into a restaurant, and every observation he or she makes is strictly from the diner's point of view. Typical of New Orleans, all the restaurants in *Creole Nouvelle* have unprepossessing facades that belie the dining experience waiting inside. Harried as they may have been, each of the chefs here graciously shared their time and knowledge with me.

I know what goes on in the kitchen and what they are doing in there, why they are doing it, and what they are using to get the food to the point where that plate is set on the table in front of you. I am not saying that this makes me wiser than the critic, some of whom are quite good, but my perspective is different. I know when shortcuts are taken—and when they are not taken. I know the effort and care that went into the preparation of many of the dishes in this book. When I look at the dish in front of me, I don't *just* have an appreciation for the appearance and flavor of the dish; I also think about the journey it underwent and all the elements that had to be coordinated to make that presentation. I have visions of the kitchen hubbub, noise and perspiring chefs and cooks, seafood orders not arriving on time from a purveyor, a sous chef being out sick, a dishwasher quitting in the middle of the shift, and all the other behind-the-scenes frenetic, controlled cacophony resulting in the appealing dish set before you in the serene, attractive dining room setting. It is my hope that, in addition to any culinary expertise you may garner from this book, the recipes and chefs in this book will engender that appreciation in you as well.

creole nouvelle

# chapter 1

# TECHNIQUES AND INGREDIENTS IN THE NEW CREOLE COOKERY

One of the main differences between home cooks and professional chefs is the fact that the latter are classically trained. All chefs share a certain corpus of knowledge to which home cooks have no real access. While it is true there are now television shows from the various professional culinary schools around the country, the shows are recipe oriented and "home cook styled." And, yes, you may buy the same large tomes that professional cooks and chefs purchase.

Yet you will hear no discussion of the "five techniques" known and understood by *all* professional chefs. This chapter deals very briefly with those five techniques. Every recipe in this book (and every other cookbook ever written) falls into one of these five techniques, as long as we are dealing with *heat* and *cooking*, not presentation.

Once you know how to 1. grill and roast (bake), 2. sauté (fry), 3. boil (poach, simmer, blanch, and steam), 4. braise (stew and pot roast), and 5. extract (soups and sauces), you will know all the fundamentals you need to cook like a professional. Each of these techniques has a specific set of procedures and a very well defined time frame for its execution. Once you grasp these few facts, you should be able to prepare just about anything. As you proceed through *Creole Nouvelle*, try to get in the habit of looking for the technique employed in any given recipe. Sautés and fried foods will have a short cooking time; braised dishes and extractions will have the longest time. Boiled dishes will be all over the map. I will help you get an idea of how to gauge cooking times for the recipes. And no recipe in this book will violate the techniques.

Most of my evening students have been busy professionals—educated cultured people who want to cook better. They always want tricks. There are no tricks. There is *only* sound technique.

*Good* home cooks throw many of the recipes that we think of as *traditional* Creole together in a slapdash fashion. The results are often disorganized, unpredictable, and unreplicable. I tell my students that I never make a move in the kitchen without a very specific end in mind and that any teacher who cannot tell them precisely *why* they do what they do is probably not worth his or her salt. Since I think Creole cookery is a very special kind of cuisine, I have crafted all the recipes to feed six to eight folks—the size group I consider ideal for a dinner party. You may simply and easily cut the recipes down if you wish to cook for fewer. In some instances, the recipes provided to me by the chefs may be for four.

## INGREDIENTS AND TERMINOLOGY

Most of the ingredients you will need to reproduce the dishes found here are available in your local supermarket or from your local fishmonger or spirit purveyor. In this section, I will not list ingredients that may be obtained in any local market around the country—just those easily found in Louisiana or more readily available to the professional chef than the home cook but maybe scarce elsewhere.

ABSINTHE: This French liqueur has been banned in the United States since around the time of World War I. It probably got a bad rap. It was thought that the wormwood in it caused brain damage. That is probably not so. Unhygienic distillation was more likely at fault. Absinthe got its name from the scientific name of wormwood (*Artemisia absinthium*). When you peruse the older Creole cookbooks, you will find absinthe as a frequent ingredient. You may substitute just about any anise- or licorice-flavored liqueur. At one time, there was a great ritual around the drinking of absinthe involving dripping the absinthe on sugar and ice. While the Sazerac Bar in the Hotel Roosevelt did not create this cocktail, "The Sazerac" is based on this ritual. Absinthe (quite safe now, by the way) is now being made in various places in the world.

ANDOUILLE: (an-due-ee) While thought of mostly as a Cajun ingredient, the Creoles also incorporated—and still do—this sausage in their cookery. The sausage is a spicy, smoked pork sausage that could be of German or possibly French (Brittany) origin.

ARTICHOKES: Yes, I know you know what an artichoke is. It is a thistle, and all of them marketed in the United States come from California today. I have had folks ask me why Louisiana cookery is rife with artichoke recipes. It was introduced to Louisiana long before it went to California and was widely grown there commercially until World War II.

BOUDIN BLANC: (boo-dan blanh) This is a white sausage made in Louisiana as well as France, where it is different. The French version is not as hearty as its Louisiana cousin. Pork and rice are the base ingredients in Louisiana, with usually a little greenery added. In France, chicken is added, and rice flour replaces the rice. This is a "fresh"—not smoked—sausage. When Louisianians talk of "Boudin," this and not the blood sausage discussed next, is almost invariably what they are talking about.

BOUDIN NOIR: (boo-dan nywah) This is an ancient French sausage made today in Louisiana. It is literally a "blood sausage," a dark sausage incorporating the blood of the pig. Several New Orleans chefs—particularly those with a French orientation—are featuring it in their cuisine.

BOUQUET GARNI: This may be almost any combination of herbs, spices, and vegetables, either tied together or bound in cheesecloth. It usually includes parsley, thyme, bay leaves, basil leaves, and celery.

CHOUPIQUE CAVIAR: (shoo-pick) Most people would know this fish by the name bowfin or cypress bass. Costing only a fraction of the price of its distant relative, sturgeon caviar, many think it compares favorably with Russian Sevruga caviar. Several thousand pounds of this caviar are produced in Louisiana every year. It has found favor with several Creole chefs.

CLARIFIED BUTTER: This is an ingredient I use almost daily. Butter contains milk-fat solids, liquid butterfat, and water. Two of these will not survive high heat. The water will evaporate, and the milk-fat solids will burn. Melt the butter slowly until it is completely liquefied. Skim the foam (mostly water with some of the lighter milk-fat solids) from the top. Carefully pour off the clear liquid butterfat, leaving the heavier milk-fat solids behind in the bottom of your pot.

COURT-BOUILLON: (coor-boo-yahn) A poaching or boiling liquid used most often with shellfish, it employs various seasonings, spices, and herbs.

FILÉ POWDER: (fee-lay) Filé powder is made from dried and ground sassafras leaves. Occasionally, dried thyme will be added as well. Used as both a seasoning and a thickening agent in gumbo, it has a distinctly pungent taste and aroma. Filé should never be added to a pot of gumbo while it is cooking but rather should be added at the end when the cooking is finished. Once you have added the powder, never bring the gumbo to a boil again, or you end up with something bearing a closer resemblance to Silly String than anything edible.

FLATIRON STEAK: Most of the chuck (shoulder) on a steer is tough and must be braised or boiled. A fairly new commercial cut of beef, this cut is the exception. It is a *very* tender muscle. The steak was brought to market as a result of research by the Universities of Nebraska and Florida. While we have known for years that this tender muscle was in the chuck, it has not been easy to bring it to market.

GINGER: The best way to mince ginger is to peel a finger of the root and slice it across the grain into very thin disks—approximately ⅛ inch thick. Place the disks near the edge of your table or counter and smash them by placing the blade of a wide knife on top of them and firmly hitting it with your hand. This will totally eliminate the problem of "stringiness." The ginger virtually minces itself.

HANGER STEAK: The French call this *onglet*. It is also known as the "hanging tender" and consists of two small muscles that support the diaphragm—just below the loin. At the time of this writing, only specialty butchers can provide you with either the flatiron or the hanger steaks.

HERBSAINT: Herbsaint is an anise-flavored liqueur from New Orleans. It probably had its origins in the 1850s as a cheaper domestic alternative to the absinthe that was quite trendy with the intellectual set of the day. When the U.S. government banned absinthe in 1912, many chefs began to substitute Pernod in recipes that called for absinthe. Others replaced it with the domestic Herbsaint at about half the cost.

LAGNIAPPE: (lan-yap) Mark Twain may be responsible for this word traveling up the Mississippi from New Orleans. It means "a little something extra." In *Life on the Mississippi*, Twain says it is "a nice, limber, expressive word." The Spanish brought it to New Orleans from the *Quechua* language–the tongue spoken by the Incas. They took the Quechua word *nyap* and put a *la* in front of it. And then it looks like the French Creoles decided to spiff up the spelling a little. Look for the "Lagniappe" boxes throughout the book. I throw in a little something extra in them.

MANCHEGO: (man-chay-go) Probably the best-known Spanish cheese, it is made from sheep's milk. It is the cheese of La Mancha.

MIREPOIX: (mere-uh-pwah) This is a mixture of root vegetables uniformly cut into a medium dice. Most often when we use the term, we are referring to carrots, celery, and onions, although parsnips and rutabagas are sometimes included. This mixture is ever present in professional kitchens and not only is a key element in many soups, stocks and stews but also serves as "bedding" material for roasts.

MIRLITON: (mere-li-ton) A subtropical squash sometimes called "alligator pear" in Louisiana. Also known as "chayote." Both the texture and the flavor are quite similar to zucchini.

MT. TAM CHEESE: Mount Tamalpais is a "mountain" in Marin County just north of San Francisco. I could see it from Sausalito when I worked as a chef there. Mt. Tam cheese is a triple-cream, rich, organic cow's milk cream cheese made by Cowgirl Creamery in Marin County. Two former Bay Area chefs, Sue Conley and Peggy Smith, founded this artisan cheese company. Chef Anne Kearney of Peristyle is a big fan of their cheeses.

MUSCOVY DUCK: (musk-uh-vee) This breed has been available in Europe for quite some time. The duck you are most likely to find in your local supermarket is the Pekin duck. Chefs who prefer the Muscovy usually cite that it is a leaner duck and that all such ducks bred in this country are naturally farm raised. One may buy breasts, legs, whole duck, and various processed specialties. Hens brought to market average about 4 pounds, while drakes can be quite large, over 7 pounds. Originally from South America, this breed is the only domestic breed not derived from the mallard. As time goes on, you will see this duck become available nationally.

PEYCHAUD'S BITTERS: (pay-shows) You will see this in the occasional Creole recipe. You are more likely to see it in a cocktail, though. New Orleanians lay claim to inventing the cocktail. An apothecary named Antoine Amadie Peychaud set up shop in the French Quarter in the early 1800s. Somewhere around 1830, he whipped up a toddy consisting of brandy, aromatic bitters (his own recipe), and a little water and sugar. A potable purveyor on Exchange Alley, Sewell Taylor, picked up this beverage for his clientele and is responsible for the Sazerac cocktail. One of his bartenders began coating the glasses for the cocktail with absinthe. This bar moved to the Hotel Roosevelt in 1949.

PERNOD: (pear-know) This is actually half the name of a French company as well as a spirit. The company, Pernod Ricard, is the principal producer of anise, star anise, and licorice-flavored beverages on the planet. They distill Ricard (mostly sold in Europe), Pernod and Pastis 51. Although a lot of Americans seem to shun these liqueurs, Pernod Ricard is selling nine million cases a year worldwide. Somebody besides me likes them. I used to sit at the bar in Vesuvio's, often with a book I had bought across the alley at City Lights Bookstore, in North Beach and sip Pernod in the late 1960s. Most New Orleans chefs now use Herbsaint for this flavor element in their cuisine.

PLAQUEMINES PARISH OYSTERS: (plack-uh-mun) Plaquemines Parish oysters are a little saltier than other oysters from the Gulf of Mexico, and their quality is unmatched. This parish is southeast of New Orleans and is a veritable font of seafood delicacies, being home to several crawfish, shrimp, soft-shell crab, and alligator farms. Do not confuse the parish with the small town of Plaquemine, the parish seat of Iberville Parish, a few miles from Baton Rouge.

STEEN'S CANE SYRUP: This syrup has been an ingredient in Creole recipes for nearly 100 years. It comes in a garish yellow can or with a yellow label on the bottle and is the Louisiana equivalent of maple syrup in the north. They also make an interesting cane vinegar should you choose to experiment.

SWEAT: Means to cook in hot fat without browning (that would be sautéing) until whatever it is you are sweating "exudes its juices."

TASSO: A cured and cold-smoked spicy pork shoulder, a common Creole recipe ingredient.

# FOOD "TOOLS": STOCKS AND SAUCES

Many of the dishes in the book require *some* knowledge of how to make sauces and stocks. These are "liquid food" and, if you will pardon the pun, the professional chef's stock in trade. One cannot do any really serious cooking without knowledge of these few basics: white and brown stocks, the basic mother sauces (velouté, béchamel, hollandaise, and mayonnaise, the "egg emulsion" sauces), Espagnole (brown sauce), and tomato sauce. We will, of course, learn how to make roux. None of the recipes in this book call for the Espagnole, so we will save it for another day.

## STOCKS

There are, in fact, just two basic stocks—brown stock and white stock. Each may be made with many different foodstuffs. But the technique remains basically the same for each whatever the base. Stock, or water, which has been infused with flavor from meat or fish, with vegetables and herbs added, is the basis of two of the mother sauces and an infinite variety of soups and stews and, when reduced, an addition to many sauté dishes. It is not absolutely essential that you make a stock to make a sauce. There are now on the market some excellent "bases," such as "fish base," "beef base," and "chicken base" (these "bases" are essences of the food mentioned and usually come in the form of a paste), to which one need only add water to create a stock. There are also canned stocks and broths available in nearly every supermarket in the country. I have found that most bouillon cubes are too salty for my taste.

## Making Stock

Making one's own stock is incredibly simple and not at all time consuming, and the chances are excellent that you already have most of the ingredients in your kitchen. Here are a very few simple rules for making stock of any kind:

1. *Always* begin with cold water. The cold water will extract both flavor and nutrition from the ingredients. Do not boil the stock, except for the moment you bring it to the boil before reducing it to a simmer. Boiling will tend to reincorporate the albumen we want to skim off.

2. *Never* salt stock. There are two reasons for this. If there is no salt in the water, the natural salts occurring in the foods that carry much of the flavor will migrate to the liquid. Also, some stocks are reduced to 25% (or less) of their original volume. If the stock had the proper amount of salt at its full volume, it will be inedible when reduced.

3. Always roast the bones, trimmings, vegetables, and so on for a brown stock.

4. The best stocks will result from a ratio of approximately 2 pounds of bones and trimmings for each gallon of water.

5. Leave the skins, leaves, and tops on vegetables to obtain the maximum flavor and nutrition from them.

# basic white stock: chicken stock

Chicken stock is the most common and versatile of the white stocks, so I will use it in my illustration. Note that when we wish to "extract" flavor and nutrition from solid food in a liquid we do not salt the liquid and we begin with a cold liquid. You may, of course, use whole chickens to make stock. In the restaurant we make use of trimmings.

| INGREDIENT | QUANTITY | METHOD |
|---|---|---|
| Chicken bones, skin, etc. | 4 lb. | 1. Place chicken in stockpot. |
| Onion, medium | 1 or 2 | 2. Wash and roughly chop onion, carrot, and celery. Do not peel vegetables. Include celery leaves. Add to stockpot. |
| Carrots | 2 | |
| Celery | 4 ribs | 3. Add parsley stems. |
| Parsley | 12 stems | 4. Smash garlic cloves with the side of your knife. Add. |
| Garlic cloves | 2 | |
| Bay leaves | 4 | 5. Add spices. |
| Thyme, whole | 1 tsp. | 6. Cover with cold water. |
| Peppercorns, black, whole | 8–12 | 7. Bring to a boil, skim, and reduce heat to simmer and cook for 2 hours. |
| Water, cold | 2 gal. | |
| | | 8. Strain through china cap. If you have the luxury of making the stock a day ahead and refrigerating it overnight, you will have a much easier time removing the fat. |

**LAGNIAPPE** - *Veal stock* will take about 4 hours to extract the flavor and nutrition from the bones. Simply substitute veal bones for the chicken. *Fish* or *shellfish stock* requires only 30 to 45 minutes. Fish stock is made with fish heads, bones, and trimmings left after filleting. Shellfish stock may be made with shrimp shells or lobster shells (cooked or uncooked) or with the trimmings or shells of whatever shellfish may be involved in the dish. *Vegetable stock* takes about the same time.

# basic brown stock

Yes, I know this is a large quantity for the home. Glance down at item 7 under "Method." It is worthwhile to make large quantities of anything that takes so long to make. You may freeze it. You may keep it in the refrigerator for two or three days; if you bring it out and boil it for 20 minutes every two or three days, it will last for weeks. Or, alternatively, you may just cut the recipe in half.

| INGREDIENT | QUANTITY |
|---|---|
| Beef and or veal bones, sawed or cracked | 10 lb. |
| Onions, medium, roughly chopped | 2 |
| Carrots, roughly chopped | 4 |
| Tomato purée | 6 oz. |
| Celery stalks, roughly chopped | 4 |
| Garlic cloves, smashed | 4 |
| Whole black peppercorns | 12 |
| Thyme, whole | 1 tbsp. |
| Cloves | 6 |
| Bay leaves | 6 |
| Parsley | 2 or 3 sprigs |
| Water | 5 gal. |

## METHOD

1. Have the butcher or your purveyor crack the bones with a cleaver or saw. (Reducing the size and opening the bones will enable you to extract the maximum flavor and nutrition from them.)

2. Place the bones in a pan large enough to hold the bones and vegetables and roast in a 450° oven for about 30 minutes.

3. Add the vegetables and herbs and spices to the pan and continue to roast for an additional 30 minutes.

4. Place the bones and vegetables in a pot large enough to hold both them and the water.

5. Bring the water to a boil and reduce to a simmer.

6. Skim the stock.

7. Simmer for 6 to 10 hours.

# court-bouillon

The "court" in this instance just means a "short," or quick, bouillon. The following will be enough to boil 5 pounds of shrimp, crabs, or crayfish. Or it may be used to poach any of the stronger-flavored fish.

| INGREDIENT | QUANTITY |
|---|---|
| Celery, roughly chopped | 4 stalks |
| Cloves | 12 |
| Thyme, whole | 1 tbsp. |
| Bay leaves | 6 |
| Allspice, whole | 1 tsp. |
| Mace | 1 tsp. |
| Red pepper, crushed | 1 tsp. |
| Peppercorns, black | 1 tsp. |
| Parsley | 2 or 3 sprigs |
| Cumin | ½ tsp. |
| Water | 6 qt. |
| Salt | 2 tsp. |

**METHOD**

1. Combine all ingredients and simmer for 15 minutes.

2. Add shrimp, crabs, or crayfish and boil until done. The large shrimp will take about 3 to 4 minutes, blue crabs 7 to 8 minutes, and Dungeness crabs 10 to 12 minutes. The crayfish should boil for only 5 to 6 minutes.

# SAUCES

These first four sauces here are what we call "mother sauces." By that we mean sauces that are considered essential in the repertoire of any chef and that also may be used to make compound sauces. For instance, the brown mother sauce (Espagnole—usually turned into a demi-glace) and both the white mother sauces (béchamel and velouté) are relatively bland as made and are actually meant to be used in combination with additional ingredients. The hollandaise and tomato sauces stand well on their own, but both have many variations and offspring.

These mother sauces are all sauces that we make ahead and then use frequently with quick, à la minute (very fast) preparations on the cooking line or in the pantry (cold-food area of the kitchen).

Three of the mother sauces, including the Espagnole, require a roux.

## A Few Words about Roux

Roux is a mixture of fat and flour, cooked together. While one may use just about any fat generally recognized as safe, butter is the fat of preference for roux in nearly all classical cookery. For certain applications, olive oil or peanut oil might be chosen.

The word roux means "reddish brown." While the original roux was undoubtedly brown, roux should be thought of in terms of shades. As long as we are making roux with butter, there is no true "white" roux. When we speak of "white" roux, we are talking about a roux in which the flour has not been allowed to color. That "white" roux will actually be a pale blond color. The next gradation will be a medium blond, followed by a light brown, medium brown, and, finally, dark brown.

Roux, primarily used as a thickener, actually has three functions:

1. Roux is used to thicken sauces, soups, and stews.
2. Roux provides heartiness and depth of flavor in a given dish.
3. Roux may be a "binder." For example, certain soups (such as lentil or split pea) have a tendency to stratify in the pot, with the heavier ingredients sinking to the bottom. A little roux added to the soup prevents this.

> **LAGNIAPPE** - As long as your roux is to be a blond one, you may make it with *whole butter*. But if you wish to make a *brown roux* of any shade, *you must use clarified butter or cooking oil*, such as peanut or olive oil. The mistake that most home cooks make is attempting to make a colored roux with whole butter. The milk-fat solids in the butter burn, and, consequently, the roux is ruined. There is no such thing a *partially* burned roux. I have seen many home-style cookbooks enjoin the cook to combine butter and oil for this purpose. It doesn't work. Even if one raises the flash point of the "liquid" cooking oils, the solids will still burn.

# béchamel

This sauce is named after Louis de Bechameil, Marquis de Nointel, who was Steward of the Royal Household under King Louis XIV. The sauce was probably conceived in the royal kitchen and given the Marquis' name to glorify him. While the sauce has undergone some small transformations since its conception in the 17th century, it is still nothing more than a mixture of roux and milk. The original béchamel was probably a mixture of the velouté and the béchamel as made today.

| INGREDIENT | QUANTITY |
|---|---|
| Butter, unsalted | 4 oz. |
| Flour, all-purpose, unbleached | 4 oz. |
| Milk, whole | 2½ c. |
| Salt | To taste |
| Pepper, white | To taste |
| Nutmeg | Pinch |

## METHOD

1. Combine the butter and flour in a saucepan. Cook over medium heat, whisking constantly with a wire whip until the flour smells cooked (it will have virtually no smell until it is cooked) and a light golden color is achieved. Remove from heat. You just made a blond roux.

2. Bring the milk to a simmer in another saucepan.

3. Using the whip, thoroughly incorporate the roux into the milk.

4. Add salt, pepper, and nutmeg.

5. Strain the sauce to remove any little bits of flour that may not have been thoroughly incorporated.

6. Dot the top of the sauce with a little butter and set aside until needed.

# hollandaise sauce

This "egg emulsion" sauce gives rise to the fewest derivative sauces—probably because it is so good as it is. A 19th-century French sauce, the name is actually much newer. The original name was probably "*Sauce Isigny*," from the name of a village in Normandy famous for its butter. During World War I, France had to import much of its butter from Holland. This gave birth to "hollandaise" sauce.

| INGREDIENT | QUANTITY |
|---|---|
| Egg yolks | 4 |
| Lemon juice | 2 tbsp. |
| Cayenne pepper | To taste |
| Dijon mustard | 1 tsp. |
| Salt | ½ tsp. |
| Butter, melted, hot, unsalted | 16–20 oz. |

## METHOD

1. Combine egg yolks, lemon juice, cayenne, Dijon, and salt in a stainless mixing bowl and beat thoroughly with wire whip.

2. Place bowl on low heat, directly on the burner on the stove.

3. Whisk the egg mixture constantly until the mixture begins to set. When you can begin to see the bottom of the bowl through the mixture, the eggs are beginning to set.

4. Remove from heat immediately and begin incorporating the butter in a slow, steady stream. If you notice at this point that you don't seem to have enough hands to simultaneously hold the bowl, add the butter *and* use the whisk, try this: dampen a kitchen towel, form it into a small circle, and set the mixing bowl on it.

5. Continue adding butter until a smooth, sauce-like consistency is achieved. Egg yolks vary somewhat in their ability to absorb fats. The Platonic ideal we seek here is a balance between the egg and butter flavors.

**LAGNIAPPE** - Although you will probably never see another cookbook designed for the serious home cook in which you are enjoined to place the eggs directly on the heat as we do in the above method, do not be afraid. You may "break" the sauce once or twice (in which case you will have delicious lemon- and mustard-flavored scrambled eggs in a rich butter sauce), but this technique will give you a much more stable emulsion than most other manners of making this sauce.

That being said, the emulsion is never so stable that you may abuse it. Once you have made the sauce, you may not subject it to more fire or refrigeration. The sauce must be kept in a warm place until you are ready to serve it. I usually place it on the shelf on top of my stove. Also, once you expose egg yolks to the air, they will tend to form a crust in short order. Leave a wire whip in the bowl and whisk the sauce every now and then if you are not serving it immediately.

# tomato sauce
## (salsa di pomodori; sauce tomate, au maigre)

My version of this mother sauce tends more toward the Italian or southern French notion of tomato sauce, as is evidenced by the use of the fresh basil. Although the Italians did give us this "elder stateswoman" of the mother sauces, it did not make its appearance until 200 years after Columbus stumbled on the New World. We have lost its creator but are eternally grateful to the anonymous chef.

| INGREDIENT | QUANTITY | METHOD |
|---|---|---|
| Onion, finely diced | 1 medium | 1. Cook onion, carrot, and garlic in olive oil over low heat in a saucepan until just softened, about 5 minutes. Do not brown. |
| Carrot, finely diced | 1 medium | |
| Garlic, minced | 1 tbsp. | |
| Olive oil, virgin or extra virgin | ¼ c. | 2. Add tomatoes, purée, basil, salt, and pepper. |
| Tomatoes, Roma, medium, peeled and seeded | 8 | 3. Simmer, covered, for about 45 minutes. |
| | | 4. Pass the sauce through a food mill or process in the food processor. |
| Tomato purée | ½ c. | |
| Basil, fresh | 2 tbsp. | 5. Use or refrigerate. |
| Salt | ½ tsp. | |
| Pepper, black, freshly ground | To taste | |

**LAGNIAPPE** - Use fresh tomatoes only if you are able to obtain truly vine-ripened Roma tomatoes or some of the meaty, vine-ripened heirloom tomatoes. Otherwise, use the canned Italian tomatoes. Trust me here. Most of the tomatoes you buy in the supermarket have little or no flavor and will *not* make a good tomato sauce. The canned Romas (Italian) will have already been peeled and will have very few seeds.

# velouté

*Time investment: Your time*—Five minutes to make the roux and 5 minutes to incorporate the roux in the stock and strain. This assumes that you already have the stock on hand. *Dish time*—Five minutes to simmer.

This is the second of the classic white sauces. You will need some of the white stock you already learned how to make. There's no historical anecdote involved here. "Velouté" simply means velvety or smooth.

| INGREDIENT | QUANTITY | METHOD |
|---|---|---|
| Butter, unsalted | 4 oz. | 1. Melt the butter in a fry pan or a saucepan on medium heat. |
| Flour, all-purpose | 4 oz. | 2. Add the flour and incorporate thoroughly with a wire whip. |
| White stock, hot | 1 qt. | 3. Simmer the roux until the flour has cooked and has just begun to color slightly. |
| Salt | To taste | 4. Add the roux to the stock and thoroughly incorporate. |
| Pepper, white | To taste | 5. Add salt and white pepper to taste. Simmer 5 minutes. |
| | | 6 Strain through a sieve or china cap. |
| | | 7. If the sauce is not to be used immediately, dot the top with butter. |

## ADDITIONAL SAUCES

There are food writers out there who would have us believe that the word barbecue comes to us from the French *barbe a queue*, which translates as "beard to tail." Several 18th- and 19th-century New World travelers and writers mentioned *"barbacoa"* or *"borbecus"*—raised wooden frameworks used as beds or for smoking meats. This linguistic ancestry seems much more likely, given the "racks" or grids on which we "barbecue."

*barbecue sauce*

| INGREDIENT | QUANTITY | METHOD |
|---|---|---|
| Onions, yellow, minced | 2 | 1. "Sweat" onions, garlic, and ginger until just soft in the peanut oil in a saucepan over medium heat. |
| Garlic, finely minced | 12 cloves | |
| Fresh ginger, finely minced | 2 tbsp. | 2. Raise heat, add chile powder, and sauté about 60 seconds. |
| Peanut oil | ½ c. | |
| Cayenne | 1 tbsp. | 3. Dissolve dry mustard in 1 cup of the red wine. |
| Chile powder | 4 tbsp. | 4 Add all remaining ingredients to pan and thoroughly incorporate. |
| Catsup | 6 c. | |
| Dry mustard | 3 tbsp. | 5. Bring to a boil and reduce to a simmer. Simmer about 15 minutes. |
| Dry red wine | 2 c. | |
| Apple cider vinegar | 1 c. | |
| Apple juice | ½ c. | |
| Brown sugar | 1 c. | |
| Paprika | 5 tbsp. | |
| Soy sauce | 1 c. | |
| Tabasco | To taste | |
| Pepper, black | 1 tsp. | |

**LAGNIAPPE** - For a marinade or "basting" sauce, dilute 1 cup of barbecue sauce with 3 cups of water. For chicken, fish, or shellfish, add ½ cup of lemon juice to barbecue sauce.

# béarnaise sauce

This sauce is a derivative of the mother sauce Hollandaise. Many think that it derives its name from Béarn, a historical region and former province of southwestern France in the western Pyrenees. There is strong evidence that it was named after King Henry IV of France, who was known as "The Great Béarnais." The Basques do not use a great deal of butter in their cookery, rendering any claim that Béarn might have to this sauce feeble. Those ingesting a well-made Béarnaise are not likely to be terribly concerned with its origins anyway.

| INGREDIENT | QUANTITY |
|---|---|
| Shallots, minced | 1 tbsp. |
| Vinegar, red wine | 2 tbsp. |
| Pepper, black, coarsely ground | ½ tsp. |
| Tarragon | 1 tbsp. |
| Lemon juice | 1 tbsp. |
| Egg yolks | 3 |
| Butter, unsalted, melted, warm | 12 oz. |
| Salt | To taste |

## METHOD

1. Combine shallots, vinegar, pepper, tarragon, and lemon juice in a nonreactive (glass, stainless, enamel, or anodized aluminum) sauté or saucepan.

2. Place on high heat and reduce until about 1 tablespoon of liquid remains. (If you have used a thick-bottomed pan, you might want to remove it from the heat a little early since the heat retained by the pan will continue the reduction process.)

3. Some chefs will strain the sauce at this point, having captured the essence of the flavors in a liquid form. We prefer to leave the shallots and tarragon in the sauce.

4. Cool the reduction slightly and, using a wire whip, thoroughly combine it with the egg yolks in a stainless mixing bowl.

5. Place the bowl over low heat and whisk constantly with a wire whip until the mixture begins to thicken and the bottom of the bowl becomes visible through the mixture.

6. Remove from heat and, using a ladle, immediately begin incorporating the butter with a wire whip—slowly at first, more rapidly as you go on.

7. Taste for salt and add as needed.

# beurre blanc

This is a "sauce" that one will not find in many cookbooks, although I am beginning to see it more and more. Yet it is a basic tool in the repertoire of any chef who prepares French or Creole cuisine or seafood. This sauce is so lush as to approach decadence. It's good. It's also quick and simple. I know of no better sauce with fish.

| INGREDIENT | QUANTITY |
|---|---|
| White wine vinegar | ½ c. |
| Dry white wine | ½ c. |
| Lemon juice | 1 tbsp. |
| Shallots, finely minced | 1 tbsp. |
| Salt | ½ tsp. |
| Pepper, white, ground | ¼ tsp. |
| Butter, unsalted, very cold | 1 lb. |

## METHOD

1. Place the vinegar, wine, lemon juice, shallots, salt, and pepper in a nonreactive (glass, stainless, enamel, or anodized aluminum) sauté or fry pan.

2. Place pan on high heat and reduce until only 1 or 2 tablespoons of the liquid are left. Reduce the heat to low.

3. Cut the butter into tablespoon-size pieces and begin adding to the pan gradually. Incorporate with a wire whip, agitating constantly. The trick here: *Don't permit the mixture to boil.* If you place your butter in the freezer for an hour or two before you make the sauce, it will help you control the temperature. You may also control the temperature by moving the pan on and off the heat as needed.

4. When all the butter has been added, check the seasoning and hold in a warm place until you are ready to serve.

# cocktail sauce

This is a quick and easy cocktail sauce. I like it with boiled shrimp, raw oysters, and just about any deep-fried shellfish.

| INGREDIENT | QUANTITY |
|---|---|
| Chili sauce (you can buy this) | 24 oz. |
| Fresh horseradish | To taste |
| Lea & Perrins Worcestershire sauce | 1 tsp. |
| Tabasco | To taste |
| Lemon juice | ¼ c. |
| Green onions, minced | 1 bunch |
| Parsley, minced | ½ c. |
| Water | ½ c. |

## METHOD

1. Place the chili sauce in a non-reactive bowl.

2. Peel horseradish and grate—a microplane is good for this. I mention "to taste" above. I personally like at least ½ cup of fresh horseradish in my cocktail sauce.

3. Mix in all other ingredients and chill for at least 30 minutes. (The water thins the cocktail sauce to a dipping sauce consistency.)

4. Mix all ingredients together.

# creole sauce

Although it employs many identical ingredients, my Creole sauce is very different from the traditional Creole sauces one sees in New Orleans. The dishes with which this sauce is most often used, Chicken Creole and Shrimp Creole, seemed to "age" if one made them ahead in the restaurant. In other words, the dishes would lose their fresh food appeal and not be at their peak when served. Additionally, the shrimp would become tough if held too long after preparation.

Having tried several solutions to these problems—none of which thrilled me—I asked myself one day, What is the "freshest" sautéed or fried food around?

I had one thought: The Oriental stir-fry. So I began experimenting. I tried oil as a base. I didn't like it. After many attempts, I came up with this recipe. I've been making it for many years now and have received no complaints. It is a kind of fusion of classical European and Oriental techniques.

| INGREDIENT | QUANTITY | METHOD |
|---|---|---|
| Clarified butter | 2 oz. | 1. Heat the clarified butter in a saucepan. |
| Onion, yellow, julienne | 1 medium | 2. Sweat the onion, bell pepper, and celery until soft. |
| Bell pepper, medium, julienne | 2 | 3. Add garlic, thyme, and crushed red pepper and continue cooking over medium heat. |
| Celery, sliced thinly on the bias | 2 ribs | |
| Garlic, minced | 1 tbsp. | 4. Add tomatoes, purée, and all stock except ½ cup. Simmer for 5 minutes. |
| Thyme, whole | ½ tbsp. | |
| Red pepper, crushed | 1 tsp. | 5. Add salt and pepper. |
| Tomatoes, peeled, seeded, chopped | 2 c. | 6. Thoroughly combine remaining stock (cold!) and cornstarch or arrowroot. |
| Tomato purée | ½ c. | |
| Stock, shrimp or chicken | 1 pt. | 7. Add starch mixture to the sauce and cook until translucent. |
| Salt | To taste | |
| Pepper, black, freshly ground | To taste | 8. Taste. |
| Cornstarch or arrowroot | 3 tbsp. | |
| Sugar | Pinch | |

# marchand de vin sauce

This sauce, in my take on it, while seemingly totally unrelated to the Creole sauce, actually came into existence after I struck upon that solution. I originally learned to make this sauce with a roux. The roux seemed really heavy-handed to me with the delicate applications appropriate to this sauce—Eggs Hussarde (found on page 138), for instance.

| INGREDIENT | QUANTITY | METHOD |
|---|---|---|
| Butter, unsalted | 2 oz. | 1. Melt butter in saucepan on medium heat. |
| Mushrooms, sliced | 8 oz. | 2. Add mushrooms and sweat briefly. |
| Green onions, minced | 1 bunch | 3. Add green onions. Again sweat briefly. |
| Garlic, minced | 1 tbsp. | 4. Add all other solids. |
| Beef or chicken stock | 2 c. | 5. Add stock. |
| Dry red wine | 2 c. | 6. Add 1 cup of the wine, the purée, and the Tabasco. |
| Tomato purée | ¼ c. | 7. Thoroughly combine cornstarch with remaining wine and add. |
| Cornstarch (or arrowroot) | 3 tbsp. | 8. Add salt and pepper. |
| Tabasco sauce | To taste | |
| Salt | To taste | |
| Pepper, black | To taste | |

# NEW ORLEANS SOUPS

I n this chapter, I will begin to include a few recipes from New Orleans chefs. If the format is slightly different from mine, you will have to bear with me. I do not wish to change anything in their recipes since they know where I live.

One of the areas where the older Creole restaurants excelled was in soup making. Turtle soup was de rigueur in all the older Creole restaurants. I remember fondly the version prepared at Delmonico's. Antoine's Seafood Gumbo is another that stands out in memory. Among the heartier soups in this chapter is the Purée of White Bean and Claret from Corinne Dunbar's. The Creole Nouvelle restaurants, though, are certainly no soup slouches. Bayona's Susan Spicer is justly well known for her Cream of Garlic Soup, and I think you will have to admit that Peter Vazquez's Thai Crab and Coconut Soup is decidedly out of the ordinary.

I have attempted to run the gamut here, including hot and cold; seafood, meat, poultry, and vegetable; creamy and clear; and thick and thin soups. And no discussion of New Orleans soups would be complete without gumbos.

# turtle soup au sherry

I am not exactly wild about using this dish title. I have kept it here because under this name it is a traditional soup in the older Creole restaurants. I like to stick to one language.

## INGREDIENT

| INGREDIENT | QUANTITY |
|---|---|
| Clarified butter | 16 oz. |
| Flour, all-purpose | 1 c. |
| Fresh turtle meat, cubed | 1 lb. |
| Celery, minced | 1½ c. |
| Onions, minced | 2 c. |
| Garlic, minced | 2 tsp. |
| Bay leaves | 3 or 4 |
| Fresh oregano | 1 tsp. |
| Fresh thyme | 1 tsp. |
| Salt | 1 tsp. |
| Pepper, black, freshly ground | 1 tsp. |
| Tomato purée | 1 c. |
| Stock, beef, chicken, seafood or vegetable | 2 qt. |
| Lemon juice | 2 lemons |

### THE GARNISH

| | |
|---|---|
| Dry sherry | 6–8 tsp. |
| Hard-cooked eggs, diced | 4 |
| Minced parsley | 1 tbsp. |

## METHOD

1. Place 12 ounces of the clarified butter in a saucepan and add the flour. Make a light brown roux and set aside.

2. Place remaining butter in a saucepan big enough to hold all ingredients (at least 5 quarts).

3. Cook turtle meat over high heat until it is caramelized. Add vegetables and seasonings and sweat until onion is translucent.

4. Add tomato purée, stock and lemon juice and whisk until uniform. Simmer 20 minutes.

5. Using a whisk add just enough of the roux to make the soup a thin purée.

6. Check seasoning.

7. Ladle the soup into bowls and add a teaspoon of sherry to each.

8. Garnish with the hard-cooked eggs and parsley.

# cream of garlic soup

This soup has been called a "New Orleans institution." It is a Bayona staple, and Chef Susan Spicer has been both serving it there and kind enough to share the recipe for it for many years. Just in case you missed it elsewhere, here it is again.

| INGREDIENT | QUANTITY |
|---|---|
| Onions, peeled and roughly chopped | 2 lb. |
| Garlic, peeled and chopped | 2 c. |
| Olive oil | 2 tbsp. |
| Butter | 2 tbsp. |
| Chicken stock | 1½ qt. |
| Bouquet garni (parsley stems, thyme sprigs, and bay leaf, tied together) | 1 |
| Stale French bread, torn into ½-inch pieces | 2 c. |
| Half-and-Half | 1 c. |
| Salt and pepper | To taste |

## METHOD

1. In a 1-gallon, heavy-bottomed pot, sauté onions and garlic in butter and oil, stirring frequently over low to medium heat until they turn a deep golden brown (about 30 minutes).

2. Add chicken stock and bouquet garni and bring to a boil.

3. Stir in bread cubes and simmer for 10 minutes until bread is soft.

4. Remove bouquet garni and purée the soup in a blender—be careful not to overfill the processor!

5. Strain through a medium strainer. Heat and whisk in more chicken stock if the soup is too thick.

6. Add Half-and-Half and season to taste with salt and pepper.

# chef pete's thai crab and coconut soup

This soup may look nothing like anything remotely Creole to your way of thinking—remember, I warned you about this. Open your mind to the infinite possibilities of New Orleans cookery. Chef Peter Vazquez of Marisol was kind enough to share this recipe with me.

| INGREDIENT | QUANTITY |
|---|---|
| Peanut oil | 2 tbsp. |
| Red onion, thinly sliced | 3 |
| Garlic, chopped | 3 tbsp. |
| Basil, finely chopped | 1 bunch |
| Fresh ginger, minced | 2-inch piece |
| Red curry paste | 1 tbsp. |
| Pistehan shrimp fry (Proprietary spice mixture found in Asian markets) | 4 tbsp. |
| Lemongrass, thinly sliced | 1 bunch |

Sauté above ingredients over medium high heat for 10 minutes. Then add:

| | |
|---|---|
| Chicken stock (must be strong) | ½ gal. |

| | |
|---|---|
| Sambal (This is a multipurpose condiment consisting mostly of chilies, brown sugar, and salt—found in Asian markets.) | 3 tbsp. |
| Fish sauce (Asian markets, again) | ½ c. |
| Lime juice | ½ c. |

Simmer above for 10 minutes. Then add:

| | |
|---|---|
| Coconut milk | 6 cans |

*Do not boil!* Then place 2 ounces of cooked lump crabmeat in each bowl and ladle hot soup over. Enjoy!

# crawfish bisque

If you were willing to go to the Asian market to obtain all the ingredients, you may be willing to put out a little effort into executing my take on the following traditional New Orleans recipe. (Not on the same evening, of course.)

| INGREDIENT | QUANTITY |
|---|---|
| Crawfish, whole, live | 12–16 |
| Court-bouillon | 3 qt. |
| Crawfish tails, cooked, cleaned | 1 lb. |
| Onion, minced | 1 c. |
| Celery, minced | 1½ c. |
| Garlic, minced | 2 tbsp. |
| Thyme, leaf | 1 tsp. |
| Bay leaves | 4 |
| Cumin | ½ tsp. |
| Cayenne | To taste |
| Paprika | 1 tsp. |
| Salt | To taste |
| Pepper, black, freshly ground | To taste |
| Clarified butter | 1 c. |
| Tomatoes, peeled, seeded, diced | 2 c. |
| Flour, all-purpose | ½ c. |
| Parsley, minced | ¼ c. |
| Bread crumbs | 1 c. |
| Egg, large | 1 |

## METHOD

1. Boil crawfish in the court-bouillon. Remove and cool immediately so you don't overcook them.
2. Clean the crawfish by disjointing them at the juncture of the tail and head. Wash the contents of the head out under running water in the sink. Remove the tail meat from the shell and devein. Add to the pound of cooked tail meat. Set aside.
3. Sauté onion, celery, garlic, thyme, bay leaves, cumin, cayenne, and paprika in 2 ounces of the clarified butter until all vegetables are soft and beginning to brown. Add salt and pepper.
4. Add tomatoes and continue to sauté.
5. Make a light brown roux with the remaining butter and the flour.
6. Mince the crawfish tails and the shrimp.
7. Add minced crawfish and shrimp to the vegetable mixture. Thoroughly incorporate. Reserve the court-bouillon.
8. Set aside approximately 1 cup of the mixture. Cool. Add the remaining mixture to the court-bouillon in a stock pot.
9. In a mixing bowl, combine and thoroughly incorporate the bread crumbs and egg with the 1 cup of the mixture you have set aside. Stuff the crawfish heads with this mixture.
10. Using a wire whip, incorporate the roux into the court-bouillon.
11. Bring the bisque to a simmer. Heat the heads for about 5 minutes in the bisque. Garnish the bisque with the heads and parsley in the individual soup bowls.

# purée of white bean and claret soup

The small white bean tends to take longer to rehydrate than most of the other dried legumes we use. If you use the "Great Northern" bean for this soup, the difference will not be so great. I recommend the slow simmer—for about an hour and a half. Do not fret about the "claret" I have in the dish title. Any dry red wine you would drink will do nicely. Corinne Dunbar's inspired this soup.

| INGREDIENT | QUANTITY |
|---|---|
| White beans, washed, boiled, and soaked | 1 lb. |
| Dry red wine | 3 c. |
| Water | 1 gal. |
| Mirepoix | 3 c. |
| Ham, diced | 1 c. |
| Garlic, minced | 1 tbsp. |
| Thyme, leaf | 1 tbsp. |
| Bay leaves | 4 |
| Salt | To taste |
| Pepper, black, freshly ground | To taste |
| Clarified butter | ½ c. |
| Tomatoes, peeled, seeded, diced | 2 c. |
| Tomato purée | ½ c. |
| Flour, all-purpose | ¼ c. |

**METHOD**

1. Place beans and water in a stockpot.

2. In a sauté pan, sweat mirepoix, ham, and garlic along with thyme, bay leaves, salt, and pepper in 2 ounces of the clarified butter until the vegetables are just soft.

3. Add tomatoes and purée and continue to sweat for an additional 4 to 5 minutes.

4. Add all ingredients in sauté pan to stockpot and simmer for about 45 minutes. Add wine.

5. Purée all in a food processor.

6. Make a light blond roux with the remaining butter and the flour. Incorporate roux.

# creole shrimp bisque

There are dozens of versions of this classic recipe. This is my favorite. Although it is similar to the Crawfish Bisque on page 29, I include this because it is much less labor intensive and might do just as well for your purposes.

| INGREDIENT | QUANTITY |
|---|---|
| Clarified butter | 1 c. |
| Celery, diced | 1 c. |
| Onion, diced | 1 c. |
| Salt | To taste |
| Pepper, white | To taste |
| Flour, all-purpose | ½ c. |
| Garlic, minced | 1 tbsp. |
| Shrimp, 16–20 count | 3 lb. |
| Corn | 2 c. |
| Stock, shrimp or chicken | 2 qt. |
| Dry rub (see page 48) | 1 tbsp. |
| Heavy cream | 1 qt. |

## METHOD

1. Sweat celery and onion in ½ cup of the clarified butter.

2. In a separate pan, make a light brown roux with the remaining butter and the flour.

3. Add salt and pepper to the vegetables. Add minced garlic and sweat briefly.

4. Mince ½ pound of the peeled and deveined shrimp and add them to the vegetables. Cook a minute or two.

5. Add corn and continue to sweat for 5 more minutes.

6. Add stock and dry rub (see page 48) Cajun seasoning to the mixture. Add remaining peeled and deveined shrimp. Simmer for 3 minutes.

7. Add heavy cream. (If bisque is too thick, thin with a little milk.)

# creole fisherman's soup

I began making this soup in San Francisco. I would sometimes include the whole, fresh, cleaned blue crabs I got at the Housewife's Market in downtown Oakland. You may also add some of the softer fleshed fish, or scallops, but do that at the *very* end of the cooking process and serve immediately.

| INGREDIENT | QUANTITY |
|---|---|
| Onion, diced | 1 c. |
| Carrots, diced | 1 c. |
| Garlic, minced | 1 tbsp. |
| Olive oil, extra virgin | 4 oz. |
| Tomatoes, peeled, seeded, diced | 4 c. |
| Bay leaves | 2 |
| Thyme, leaf | 1 tbsp. |
| Tarragon | 2 tsp. |
| Parsley, minced | 2 tbsp. |
| Salt | To taste |
| Pepper, black, freshly ground | To taste |
| Dry white wine | 1 c. |
| Stock, fish, shellfish, or chicken | 2 qt. |
| Dijon mustard | 2–3 tbsp. |
| Firm-fleshed fish filets—rockfish, swordfish, snapper, etc., cut into 1-inch cubes | 12–16 oz. |

**METHOD**

1. Sweat the onions, carrots, and garlic in the butter or oil until just soft.

2. Add the tomatoes, bay leaves, thyme, tarragon, parsley, salt, and pepper and continue to sweat for 4 to 5 minutes over medium heat.

3. Deglaze the pan with the white wine, raise the heat, and boil the alcohol away.

4. Add the stock and Dijon mustard, bring to a boil, and reduce to a simmer; cover and simmer for about 20 minutes.

5. Add fish pieces and poach until they are cooked through.

# GUMBO

Okay, here comes the gumbo rap. You were expecting it, weren't you? One cannot write a Creole cookbook without including gumbo. The word "gumbo" has two meanings. It is a word for okra and a word for a mysterious—to outsiders—soup/stew made in southern Louisiana. Some scholars also use the word to describe the Louisiana Creole language. Current geobotanical research would seem to indicate that okra had its origins in what we now call Ethiopia.

Just as the word "Cajun" is a corruption of a corruption, "gumbo" is thought to be a corruption of a Portuguese corruption (*quingombo*) of the word *quillobo* in Congolese parlance. These linguistic things are always a little hazy by nature, as is the route by which okra reached the rest of the world. Spanish Moors knew it in the 13th century.

French colonists most likely introduced okra to Louisiana in the early 1700s. No one knows who was the first to cook gumbo or when, and there is no one way to make gumbo. Some gumbos have okra, some don't. Some have filé, some don't. Some have seafood, and, as you now are beginning to suspect, some don't. Some are made with poultry.

All the older recipes begin with a roux. I see no sound culinary reason for this. I usually add the roux later in the cooking process. Also, the Vieux Creole cooking canons would have you cook the gumbos for what I consider an unconscionable time. I have shortened cooking times to retain the freshness and individual character of the seafoods, meats, and vegetables.

I have included my new takes on four fairly typical types of gumbo, one with okra, one with filé, and two with neither.

My first and, I might add, disastrous attempt to acquire an education in the liberal arts involved a year at Louisiana State University. This was my first foray into the world of decision making, a skill that, as it turned out, would require considerable honing. In short, I was a rotten, undisciplined student. I really enjoyed the eating and drinking parts of college. I pledged a fraternity, Sigma Nu, at LSU. In this organization, I was surrounded by Cajuns from Plaquemine, Houma, Morgan City, and other bastions of Acadian culture. There were a couple of New Orleanians. But our cook seemed to have a Creole bent. While I missed a lot of what I should have been paying attention to at college, I never missed Friday lunch at the fraternity house; Mary always made a gumbo, and they were always slightly different from each other. I suppose she began setting my gumbo palate. All the gumbo recipes will make about 12 servings.

# "gombo aux crabes et chevrettes" (seafood gumbo)

I debated just where in this book I should place gumbo. Since it is food in a liquid, I opted for the soup section here. But some would call it a "stew."

In southern Louisiana, everybody and his cousin Boudreaux has a recipe for gumbo—and secrets galore. Well, let me tell you, there ain't no secrets. There is no magic here, just sound culinary technique. I will admit I did futz with this particular recipe for a couple of years before I set it to paper. It works, and at the same time it violates none of the technique guidelines we have discussed thus far.

While the title of this dish may look like bad French to you, it is in fact turn-of-the-century Creole French. I took the title (and usage) from *The Picayune Creole Cookbook*.

In the strictest sense, a dish without okra cannot be a gumbo. In reality, today there are two basic types of gumbo: gumbo containing okra as a thickening and flavor ingredient and gumbo containing filé powder, which formerly was the ground root of sassafras but now often takes the form of sassafras and thyme ground together. At one time, no real Louisiana cook would use both okra and filé in the same dish. All rules are off now. The Choctaw Indians probably introduced filé to the New Orleans market.

Gumbo is a dish that may be described as either soup if it is kept thin and meant to be served as a course early in the meal or a stew if thick and ingredient laden, meant to be served as a main course. We usually elect the latter, although the last time I ate at Herbsaint, Chef Link sent me out a very nice bowl of the former. It is served with boiled or steamed rice.

You may make this dish as a lighter soup course by entirely omitting the roux—anathema to traditional Creole cooks. I think you'll find it stands up very well as a somewhat lighter soup this way. You may even be able to eat some more food behind it. Even when I do add the roux, I do not begin with it as many Creoles do. In classical cookery, a roux is *added to a liquid—not the other way around*.

The only "trick" involved here is the stock. If we use a stock in the gumbo, the depth of flavor imparted by the stock eliminates the need to cook the seafoods and vegetables until they become a miasmic bayou.

In all the years I have been making this gumbo, I have had only one problem with it. One of my best waiters came into the kitchen on a busy winter evening. I knew something was up, as he could barely constrain himself. "Chef, a guest has a problem with the gumbo and wants to talk to you." Sigh. He told me the table number, and I reluctantly brushed myself off and headed to the dining room. The man was a solitary diner and appeared to have spent some time at a potable dispensary before electing to dine with us. "Yes, sir, just what is the problem?" I innocently queried. The waiter hovered behind me.

I am not going to attempt to reproduce the slur in the gentleman's speech. "This gumbo is too hard," he said.

"It's too hard?"

"Yep, too hard."

"You mean it's too hard to eat?" After cracking the claws and cleaning the crabs, I did put all the crab bodies with edible parts in the gumbo. I thought that was what he was referring to.

"No, it's too hard!" he sputtered, taking his knife and fork in hand and noisily attacking the hard blue crab top shell, with which I garnished the bowl of gumbo.

I gently suggested he move the shell aside and that he would then be able to eat the gumbo below.

The waiter was snickering behind me.

| INGREDIENT | QUANTITY |
|---|---|
| Okra, fresh, sliced into ¾-inch discs | 1 lb. |
| Clarified butter | 8 oz. |
| Onion, yellow, thinly sliced | 2 c. |
| Celery, sliced ½ inch thick on a 45° angle | 4–6 ribs |
| Garlic, finely minced | 2 tbsp. |
| Bay leaves | 3 or 4 |
| Thyme, whole leaf | 1 tbsp. |
| Pepper, cayenne | To taste |
| Pepper, white | To taste |
| Pepper, black | To taste |
| Salt | 1 tsp. |
| Tomatoes, peeled, seeded, chopped | 3 c. |
| Cilantro, finely minced | 1 tsp. |
| Parsley, finely minced | 2 tbsp. |
| Blue or Dungeness crabs | 2–12 |
| Shrimp, large, boiled in court-bouillon | 2 lb. |
| Court-bouillon | 1 gal. |
| Flour | ½ c. |
| Tabasco | To taste |
| Worcestershire | To taste |

**METHOD**

1. Sweat the okra in ½ of the hot clarified butter until it exudes the shiny mucilaginous substance inside. One of the secrets to making good gumbo is *cooking* this thick, slippery substance.

2. Add onions and celery and continue cooking until the onion is translucent.

3. Add garlic, thyme, peppers, and salt and continue to sauté for 2 or 3 minutes.

4. Add tomatoes, cilantro, and parsley. Sauté 1 minute.

5. Add crabs and shrimp. Sauté briefly.

6. Add stock. Bring to boil. Reduce to simmer and simmer, covered, for about 10 minutes.

7. While the gumbo is simmering, make a light brown roux with the remaining butter and the flour.

8. Using a wire whip, thoroughly incorporate the roux in the gumbo.

9. Taste for the spice balance.

10. Add Tabasco and Worcestershire to taste.

11. Simmer for an additional 10 minutes.

12. Serve over plain boiled or steamed rice.

**LAGNIAPPE** - East of the Mississippi, you are more likely to find the blue crab. Out west, the Dungeness crab is the one for you. The Dungeness is much the larger of the two, and the yield in edible meat is greater.

# gumbo z'herbes

This is yet another New Orleans dish with a story. Originally a "Lenten" (no meat) dish, it was made on Holy Thursday to be eaten the next day—Good Friday, a "fast" day. I put "fast" in quotes because in New Orleans that meant "eat less than normal." As it was first made, the dish was meatless—for Friday consumption. Of course, you may make a vegetarian version (culinary hint: omit the meat). I am including meat here.

I realize that there is a veritable slew of different kinds of "greens" in the dish. Just gather as many as you can from your local supermarket produce section. If you are in New Orleans, you will find vendors selling gumbo z'herbes greens mixtures.

Do not fret if you are forced to omit several of the types of greens. You may have difficulty locating sorrel or arugula, for instance. Also, you may add any other green vegetable tops you are able to find, such as radishes and carrots.

| INGREDIENT | QUANTITY | INGREDIENT | QUANTITY |
|---|---|---|---|
| Turnip greens | 1 bunch | Salt | 1 tbsp. |
| Mustard greens | 1 bunch | Pepper, black, freshly ground | 1 tsp. |
| Collard greens | 1 bunch | Bouquet garni | |
| Spinach | 1 bunch | 1 sprig of fresh thyme, | |
| Chicory | 1 head | 2 sprigs of fresh tarragon, | |
| Beet tops | 1 bunch | 3 bay leaves, | |
| Arugula | 1 bunch | 6 whole peppercorns, | |
| Sorrel | 1 bunch | 4 allspice berries, 4 cloves | |
| Dandelion greens | 1 bunch | Flour, all-purpose | ⅔ cup |
| Romaine | 1 head | Olive oil or clarified butter | 1 c. |
| White cabbage | ½ head | Yellow onion, medium, diced | 1 |
| Italian flat-leaf parsley | 1 bunch | Bell pepper, medium, diced | 1 |
| Water, boiling (or stock) | 1 gal. | Celery ribs, diced | 4 |
| Smoked ham hock | 1 or 2 | Garlic, minced | 1 tbsp. |
| Andouille sausage, whole | 1 lb. | Cayenne | 1 tsp. |
| | | Boiled or steamed rice (about ½ cup per serving) | 3–4 c. |
| | | Parsley, minced | 1 tbsp. |

# METHOD

1. Wash—and I mean *wash*—all greens thoroughly! You may have to rinse them several times in clear, cold water to rid them of all the sand or grit. Cut out the hard stems. Place them all in a pot with the boiling water, the ham hock, sausage, salt, pepper, and bouquet garni—the last wrapped in cheese-cloth.

2. Return the water to the boil, reduce to a simmer, and cover and simmer for about 2 hours.

3. Strain, reserving liquid, and dice all the greens. Remove the ham hock and sausage and allow them to cool enough so that you can handle them. Remove all meat from hock and dice; thinly slice the andouille. Set aside for now. Throw away the bouquet garni. Return the diced greens to the liquid. Hold. Relax—we're getting there.

4. Make a brown roux with the ½ of the oil and all the flour.

5. In a separate pan, sauté the onions, bell pepper, and celery until they are just beginning to brown.

6. Add the garlic and cayenne and remove from heat.

7. Add the onion/pepper/celery mixture to the pot with the greens and water. Bring to a simmer.

8. Using a wire whip, thoroughly incorporate the roux.

9. Place rice in soup bowls, ladle gumbo over it, and garnish with the parsley.

# tea-smoked duck gumbo filé with poached oysters

In addition to roux, the Creoles classically use two thickeners for their gumbos: okra and filé powder. Originally, the rule of thumb was okra during the growing season and filé (a dried spice) during the winter months when the okra was not available. Over time, this became so ingrained in the cooks' subconscious, I think, that it led to the notion that the two were never to be combined. Filé has a unique flavor and character. If boiled, it will become quite stringy. Always add it near the end of the cooking process and *never* return the liquid to the boil! I make the roux first and add the "trinity" to it.

I obtained the recipe for the Tea-Smoked Duck from my friend, Chinese chef Bernard Chang, who sadly is no longer with us. I enjoy the dish so much that I tried to think of other ways to use it. That is how the following recipe came about.

| INGREDIENTS | QUANTITY |
|---|---|
| Tea-smoked duck (see page 39) | 1 |
| Andouille sausage | 1 lb. |
| Tasso | ½ lb. |
| Peanut oil | 1 c. |
| All-purpose flour | 1½ c. |
| Large onions, diced | 2 |
| Celery, diced | 6–8 stalks |
| Medium bell peppers, diced | 3 |
| Smoked garlic | 1 head |
| Dry white wine | 2 c. |
| White pepper | ½ tbsp. |
| Cayenne pepper | ½ tbsp. |
| Fresh thyme leaves | 1 tsp. |
| Smoked duck stock | 3 qt. |
| Shucked oysters | 24–36 |
| Filé powder | 1 tbsp. |
| Salt and freshly ground black pepper | To taste |
| Boiled or steamed rice | 3–4 c. |

## METHOD

1. Pull duck meat from bones and dice into ½-inch cubes.
2. Make Smoked Duck Stock with bones. Substitute the duck bones and trimmings in the Chicken Stock recipe (see page 11). Add the unpeeled head of garlic to the smoker with the duck—about 1 hour before the duck will be ready.
3. Slice andouille and Tasso into ¼-inch pieces.
4. Place a thick-bottomed stockpot large enough to hold all ingredients on the stove and make a brown roux with the peanut oil and flour. Stir this all the while until you have added the liquids.
5. Add the "trinity"—the onion, celery, and bell peppers—to the roux and cook for 3 or 4 minutes.
6. Add the andouille and Tasso and caramelize.
7. Add garlic and deglaze with the wine.
8. Add remaining spices except filé. Sauté for a couple of minutes. Add stock.
9. Since you have a rich stock, this should not need to simmer for more than a few minutes.
10. Just before serving gumbo, add oysters and poach for 4 or 5 minutes.
11. Stir in filé at the last minute.
12. Place a ramekin of rice in the center of a large bowl. Ladle gumbo over.

# tea-smoked duck

I learned this dish originally as a stand-alone appetizer. Often when dining at my friend Bernard Chang's restaurant, I would have an all-appetizer meal consisting of this dish and pot stickers made by his mother.

A business associate of Bernard's faxed the recipe to me (with his permission) while Bernard was in the hospital. It was in Chinese calligraphy. Very funny. After they had a good laugh, they resent it in English.

When I speak of "smoking," I mean cooking in a smoker. This procedure is basically a "slow-roasting," indirect-heat technique. An ancient notion, for our ancestors it was a means of preserving food. Today we like the flavor the smoking infuses in our food. Various fruit and nut woods—hickory being the most popular—are used to impart subtle nuances.

| INGREDIENT | QUANTITY |
|---|---|
| Ducks, Muscovy or Pekin | 2 |
| Salt | ¼ c. |
| Peppercorns | ¼ c. |
| Saltpeter (optional) | 2 tbsp. |
| Wood chips | 1 lb. |
| Black tea leaves | 2 c. |
| Boiling water | 4 c. |
| Orange peel and lemon peel | 2 each |
| Peanut oil | 10 c. |

### METHOD

1. Thoroughly dry the ducks. Prepare the smoker.

2. Cook salt and peppercorns in a skillet over high heat for a minute or so. Cool.

3. Rub duck inside and out with salt and peppercorns. You may rest ducks in refrigerator overnight.

4. Soak wood chips in water. Place ducks on rack in smoker. Pour boiling water over the tea leaves and place them in a stainless container. Prick the skin of the ducks with a fork to aid in rendering the fat from the ducks.

5. Place wet tea leaves mixed with peels in a stainless container in the smoker between the coals and the ducks. You may also put some of the mixture directly on the coals for a stronger flavor.

6. Place some of the wood chips on the coals and close the smoker. Replenish occasionally.

7. Smoke ducks for 3 to 4 hours, turning occasionally.

8. Heat peanut oil to 350°. You may either fry the duck whole or cut into about 8 pieces before you fry it. Fry until skin is crisp and browned. Drain and pat dry.

## GUMBO YA YA

Many years ago when I lived in California, I bought a book called *Gumbo Ya Ya* at a used bookstore. Written in the 1940s, it is a compilation of old folklore and superstitions in southern Louisiana. I recommend it highly. The expression Gumbo Ya Ya means "everybody talking at once." In other words, a party. Yes, it's New Orleans.

This gumbo also reminds me of the 1970s when I had a Creole restaurant in California. I maintained strong ties to New Orleans to the extent possible at that distance. I had music on the weekends featuring, among others, Queen Ida and the Bon Temps Zydeco Band and for about a year my regular Saturday night band was Dick Oxtot's Golden Age Jazz band, a Dixieland band that also was the "house" band for the Oakland Athletics baseball games. I served a popular version of Gumbo Ya Ya at that restaurant during this era and often fed it to the bands.

# gumbo ya ya

This gumbo is not meant to be any particular thing. It is a "Ya Ya," a hodgepodge of ingredients. Still, I have never seen it without chicken, the "trinity" (bell pepper, onion, celery), and sausage. This is the other gumbo I make in the "traditional" manner—that is, I do begin with the roux and add the liquid to it.

| INGREDIENT | QUANTITY |
|---|---|
| Chickens, fryers | 2 |
| Salt | To taste |
| Pepper, black, freshly ground | To taste |
| Cayenne | To taste |
| All-purpose flour | 2 c. |
| Olive oil, extra virgin | 1 c. |
| Onions, diced | 2 c. |
| Celery, diced | 1½ c. |
| Green bell pepper, diced | 2 c. |
| Jalapeño, minced | 1 or 2 |
| Andouille sausage, sliced thinly | 1 lb. |
| Garlic, minced | 1 tbsp. |
| Chicken stock (see recipe page 11) | 2 qt. |
| Romaine lettuce, julienned | 1 small head |
| Cooked rice | 5–6 c. |

## METHOD

1. Either buy cut-up chickens or disjoint them yourself if you feel comfortable doing that. In either case, cut the breast in half crosswise to reduce its size. Dry the chicken thoroughly.

2. Combine the salt, pepper, and cayenne. Dredge the chicken in this mixture. Reserve flour mixture.

3. Get the olive oil hot over medium heat in a 5-quart pot and sauté the chicken pieces in it until they are golden brown. They will not be cooked completely through. Remove chicken.

4. Add one cup of the flour to the pan and make a medium brown roux scraping any fonds in the pan into the roux.

5. Add onion, celery, peppers, and andouille to pan. Remove from heat stirring constantly. When the mixture has cooled slightly, add garlic.

6. Add stock and incorporate thoroughly. Return pot to heat.

7. Return chicken to pot and bring to a boil, reduce to a simmer and simmer, covered, for about 30 minutes. (This will allow the flavors to blend and the chicken to finish cooking.) Add romaine and check seasoning. Simmer an additional 10 minutes.

8. Using a timbale or a ramekin, place rice in a soup bowl and ladle gumbo around it.

# gazpacho

Here's a "Creole" version of the traditional Spanish gazpacho, thanks to Chef Peter Vazquez of Marisol.

| INGREDIENT | QUANTITY |
|---|---|
| Onion, small, sweet, quartered | 1 |
| Red bell pepper, seeded, quartered | 1 |
| Cucumbers, medium, scrubbed and coarsely chopped | 2 |
| Zucchini, coarsely chopped | 3 |
| Celery, coarsely chopped | 1 rib |
| Garlic cloves, large, peeled | 4 |
| Tomatoes, large, fresh, ripe, quartered | 2 |
| Tomato juice or canned whole tomatoes with their juice | 3 c. |
| Fresh basil, chopped | 2 tbsp. |
| Salt and pepper | To taste |
| Balsamic or red wine vinegar | 2 tbsp. |
| Olive oil | 3 tbsp. |
| Hot sauce (optional) | |

## METHOD

1. Place the onion, pepper, cucumbers, zucchini, garlic, and fresh tomatoes in a food processor; process until finely chopped. Add the tomato juice, basil, salt, pepper, vinegar, and olive oil and hot sauce (if desired). Taste for seasoning.

2. Chill for at least 1 hour before serving. Garnish with finely chopped cucumber, whole basil leaves, sour cream, or lump crabmeat.

**LAGNIAPPE** - If you want thinner soup, use more tomato juice. For thicker soup, use all fresh tomatoes and omit the juice entirely.

# lentil soup with andouille

While we still think of them mostly as a soup ingredient, lentils are making inroads into American cuisine. Cultivated for at least 10,000 years, they are nutritious and versatile. The Spanish and Portuguese introduced them to the New World in the 16th century. This is a great chilly-weather soup.

| INGREDIENT | QUANTITY |
|---|---|
| Lentils, rinsed, boiled, and soaked | 1 lb. |
| Stock, beef or chicken | 3 qt. |
| Mirepoix | 2 c. |
| Olive oil | ¼ c. |
| Garlic, minced | 1 tbsp. |
| Leeks (if available), washed and diced | 1 c. |
| Andouille, thinly sliced | 1 c. |
| Potatoes, peeled and diced | 1 c. |
| Oregano, whole | 1 tbsp. |
| Bay leaves | 3 |
| Thyme, leaf | 1 tsp. |
| Tomatoes, peeled, seeded, and chopped | 2 c. |
| Salt | To taste |
| Pepper, black, freshly ground | To taste |
| Parsley, chopped | ¼ c. |

## METHOD

1. Place lentils in stock and bring to a simmer.

2. In a sauté pan, sweat mirepoix in olive oil over medium heat until vegetables are soft.

3. Add garlic to mirepoix.

4. Turn up heat and add sausage, potatoes, oregano, bay leaves, and thyme and continue to sauté.

5. Add tomatoes to sauté pan. Add salt and pepper.

6. Add all vegetables and spices to pot with lentils and simmer, covered for about 45 minutes.

7. Add parsley and serve.

# SANDWICHES, SALADS, AND STARTERS

New Orleans has several special sandwiches. I do not teach my students how to make very many sandwiches, as I presume most are able to make a sandwich. However, I do consider the couple of sandwiches I have included here worthy of note.

Over the past couple of decades or so, the culinary waters have become murky as to just what is a salad and what is an appetizer. I have no problem with this muddying, just as long as the starter is not too filling or cloying.

In this chapter, I have included many recipes from our five chefs. The earlier courses in the meal tend to be lighter, and many of today's diners will graze over an array of appetizers instead of eating a complete meal.

# crabmeat and zucchini phyllo turnovers

Many thanks to Susan Spicer for giving us the following recipe. Makes 8 portions.

| INGREDIENT | QUANTITY |
|---|---|
| **CRABMEAT MIXTURE** | |
| Olive oil | 2 tbsp. |
| Butter | 1 tbsp. |
| Onion, finely chopped | ½ c. |
| Fennel bulb, finely diced (optional) | ¼ c. |
| Minced garlic | 1 tsp. |
| Grated and squeezed zucchini | 2 c. |
| Flour | 2–3 tbsp. |
| White wine, sherry or fish stock | ¼ c. |
| Heavy cream | ½ c. |
| Crabmeat, cleaned of shells | 1 lb. |
| Dijon mustard | 1–2 tsp. |
| Freshly grated nutmeg | Pinch |
| Lemon | Squeeze |
| Salt, pepper, hot sauce | To taste |
| Scallions, finely sliced or chopped | ¼ c. |
| **TURNOVER** | |
| Phyllo dough | ½ lb. |
| Melted butter | ½ c. |
| Bread crumbs, mixed with a little freshly grated grana padano or parmesan cheese and 2 tsp. chopped parsley | ½ c. |

## METHOD

### CRABMEAT MIXTURE

1. In a medium sauté pan, heat oil and butter and, when foaming, add onion, fennel, and garlic and cook, stirring for about 4 to 5 minutes.

2. Add zucchini and stir, cooking 5 more minutes, then sprinkle with flour. Toss or stir to lightly coat vegetables with the flour.

3. Pour in the wine or sherry and mix thoroughly over medium heat. Mixture will thicken immediately.

4. Add crabmeat and mix gently, then pour in cream a little at a time to incorporate completely. Bring to a boil, then reduce heat and cook for about 3 minutes. Add a little more cream if necessary.

5. Remove from heat and stir in mustard, nutmeg, and lemon, then salt, pepper, and a dash of hot sauce to taste. Stir in scallions. Remove mixture to a platter or a baking sheet and place in refrigerator to cool.

### TURNOVER

1. Lay one sheet of phyllo vertically on a clean, dry work surface and brush lightly with melted butter, starting with the edges and working in. Lightly sprinkle with bread crumb mixture and cover with another sheet of phyllo.

2. Repeat for a total of three layers, then cut lengthwise in half and trim long edges slightly.

3. Place ⅛ of crabmeat mixture in the bottom corner of each half and roll up like a flag into triangles.

*continued*

Brush the tops with a little melted butter and sprinkle with a little bread crumb mixture.

4. Place on a baking sheet if using immediately or on a tray with parchment paper if not.

5. Repeat with the rest of the filling. Be sure turnovers are not touching on the tray, as the dough will not cook properly. To cook, place in 400° preheated oven and bake for about 10 to 12 minutes until golden brown and the dough underneath is crisp and lightly browned. Serve immediately with Tomato Ginger Jam or Lemon Chive Butter.

# tomato ginger jam

Here is my version of a Tomato Ginger Jam to serve with Susan's Turnovers.

| INGREDIENT | QUANTITY |
| --- | --- |
| Fresh Roma tomatoes | 5 lb. |
| Granulated sugar | 1½ c. |
| Lemon juice, fresh | 1½ c. |
| Garlic, fresh, thinly sliced, or chopped | ¼ c. |
| Fresh ginger, finely minced | 2 tbsp. |
| Salt | ½ tsp. |

### METHOD

1. Peel, seed, and chop tomatoes into ½-inch dice. Place in heavy enamel or stainless-lined pan with all other ingredients.

2. Bring to a boil, then reduce heat to a simmer. Cook the mixture for about 1½ hours.

3. Stir frequently to prevent scorching.

4. When jam thickens and begins to shine, it is done. Spread the jam out and cool it in the refrigerator in a shallow pan.

    You may serve it at room temperature or warm it.

**LAGNIAPPE** - For lemon chive butter: Soften ½ lb. of unsalted butter and add freshly ground black pepper, 2 tbsp. of minced or snipped chives, the seeded pulp of one lemon, and salt to taste. Cream all together.

# dry rub

Most of the things I barbecue involve two steps—a coating or "dry-marinating" in a dry rub and then, toward the end of the cooking process, the addition of a wet sauce.

Here is the dry rub I use most often. It works well with shrimp, oysters, chicken, and pork.

## JUST A LITTLE ABOUT BARBECUE

Most of the "barbecue" you will find in New Orleans involves seafood. While the rubs and sauces remain similar to what we would use with meat, the technique has nothing to do with "barbecuing," a slow-roasting cooking technique. The following dry rub works well with seafood, as does the barbecue sauce in chapter 2.

| INGREDIENT | QUANTITY | METHOD |
| --- | --- | --- |
| Cayenne pepper | ¼ c. | Combine all ingredients and, using your hands, either toss the food in the rub or rub it into the food. |
| Chili powder | ¼ c. | |
| Paprika | ½ c. | |
| Black pepper, finely ground | ½ c. | |
| Garlic powder | ¼ c. | |
| Cumin | 2 tbsp. | |
| Dry mustard | 1 tbsp. | |
| Celery salt | 3 tbsp. | |

# barbecue shrimp

Although I call the dishes that involve barbecue sauce but that are not "barbecued," "barbecue" to be precise, "barbecuing" is a slow-roasting cooking process—not cooking on a grill. That would be grilling. Nearly all the recipes one sees in New Orleans for barbecue shrimp call for shrimp still in the shell, and the cooking times are *way* too long (I have seen recipes that call for cooking the shrimp 30 minutes). This is an area where I take strong exception to the "old" way of cooking. I have tried *their* way, and it is not for me.

Unless you have a particular fondness for crustacean excrement, I strongly recommend you peel *and* devein the shrimp, but leave the last tail joint in place. "Vein" is a euphemism someone came up with years ago for "shrimp (or lobster or crawfish) intestinal tract." In addition, medium-size shrimp (21–25s or 16–20s) cook in boiling water in 2 to 3 minutes—even faster in hot fat. I hardly think that 30 minutes of cooking in any medium would do *anything* positive for the shrimp.

My version of barbecue shrimp begins as if one were making a scampi-style sauté. It ends with a deglazing with the barbecue sauce.

| INGREDIENT | QUANTITY | METHOD |
|---|---|---|
| Olive oil, extra virgin | ¼ c. | 1. Heat the oil in a fry or sauté pan until it is quite hot (nearly smoking, definitely shimmering). |
| Shrimp, peeled and deveined, medium | 2 lb. | 2. Dry the shrimp and toss them in a bowl with the dry rub. |
| Dry rub (see page 48) | 1 c. | 3. Shake off excess. |
| Flour, seasoned with salt, pepper and cayenne | 2 c. | 4. Toss shrimp in a bowl with the flour mixture. Shake off excess. |
| Garlic, minced | 1 tbsp. | 5. Add shrimp to pan and toss and stir until all are pink. |
| Dry white wine | 1 c. | 6. Add garlic and toss. |
| Barbecue sauce | 2 c. | 7. Deglaze with white wine. Reduce for about 1 minute. |
| | | 8. Deglaze with barbecue sauce. |
| | | 9. Serve in a flat-rimmed (Italian-style) soup bowl. Serve bread and butter on the side. |

## OYSTERS AND SHUCKING THEM

A British clergyman named William Butler was the first to enjoin us, in the late 16th century, not to eat oysters during the months that do not have an "r" in their names. His reasons for this were quite sound. European oysters were full of sand in the summer months—not necessarily unwholesome, just not tasty. American oysters spawn during the early summer, and some oyster lovers actually enjoy them more during this period. As the summer wears on, the oysters finish spawning and are quite exhausted and underweight. This is the time of year when they are least succulent.

A varmint called *Gonyaulax catenella*, a dinoflagellate (sounds sort of like a venereal disease transmitted by energetic, masochistic mollusks), has caused a quarantine on wild bivalve harvesting in the waters off the coast of California from May through October. This one-celled organism can cause shellfish poisoning. In Louisiana and the warmer eastern waters of the United States in recent years, the culprit most often has been *Vibrio vulnificus*.

Bacteria that like oysters (but don't especially like us) seem to thrive in warmer waters. Nearly all these bacteria are neutralized by heat, so if you plan to cook them, you have few worries. If you are a raw-oyster aficionado, as I am, stick to oysters harvested in the coldest winter months. These will be the plumpest and tastiest anyway. All oysters sold in the United States are from government-certified oyster beds.

Of the three types of oysters available in U.S. coastal waters, only two are easy to find: the Pacific, or Japanese oyster, and the Eastern, or Blue Point oyster. The "Eastern" oyster is found all up and down the Atlantic coast and in the Gulf of Mexico. Today you will find many "artisan" oysters or oysters with a geographic nomenclature attached indicative of some special culinary note or trait. Oysters like bays and estuaries, and these waterway designations often constitute the *nom de table*. The third, another West Coast oyster, the Olympia, is in short supply. The Eastern and Olympia oysters are indigenous, and the Pacific was introduced to American waters around 1930.

If at all possible, buy oysters in the shell and shuck them yourself. I have taught hundreds of students how to shuck oysters quickly and easily without wounding themselves using the following method. The large Pacific oysters show themselves to best advantage when baked. For oysters on the half shell, stick with the Eastern type or, should you be lucky enough to find them, the Olympia.

Oysters are quite high in protein, calcium, and zinc (the latter possibly accounting for their reputation as an aphrodisiac).

## SHUCKING THE EASTERN OYSTER

You will need a thick kitchen towel and an oyster knife. If you cannot figure out how to acquire those two objects, I would forget this project. Refer to the images in the first photospread.

Fold the towel a couple of times and place the oyster on half of it. Locate the "pointy" end of the oyster. This is where you will attack. Endeavor to have the deep side of the oyster shell on the bottom to retain liquid after it is opened. Look for a means of ingress—a small hole will do. Once you find a place to begin your insertion, insert the point of your oyster knife. Fold the other half of the towel up on top of the oyster to protect the hand that is not holding the knife. Here comes the most important part of this entire procedure: Do not push and twist at the same time!

Push the knife into the oyster. If it goes in easily, rotate your wrist while firmly holding the oyster against the table or counter with your off hand. Push *or* twist! Got it? You will want to push and twist if the oyster does not cooperate immediately. Don't do it! If the knife did not go in easily or cleanly with the first push, push again. Do not twist until the knife has entered the oyster. If the knife is in the oyster, the oyster will open with a simple twist of the wrist.

Once the oyster is open, check for bits of shell, mud, sand, and so on. If the battle has been particularly ferocious, you will want to rinse the oyster off under cold running water. You may keep the opened oyster in the refrigerator for a couple of days. Cover it with a damp kitchen cloth. Release the oyster from the second side of the shell only right before you are ready to eat or cook it.

# barbecue oysters

In certain areas, one may not always be able to purchase fresh oysters in the shell. Not to worry. I am going to give you two methods of making this dish. You should be able to find the fresh-shucked oysters in a jar, though. Those will be just dandy. Check the dates on the jar.

If you were able to get—and shuck—the shell oysters, sprinkle a little of the dry rub on each before you put them in the refrigerator. Let them "marinate" at least a couple of hours. Overnight is fine, too. If you have the jar oysters, drain them, dry them, and place them in a bowl with a tablespoon or so of the rub.

| INGREDIENT | QUANTITY |
|---|---|
| Eastern oysters | 3–4 dozen |
| Dry rub | As needed |
| Barbecue sauce | Approximately 2 c. |
| Flour (for the jar oysters) | 1 c. |
| Olive oil, extra virgin (for the jar oysters) | ½ c. |
| Rock salt (for the shell oysters) | 6 c. |

## METHOD

1. Preheat oven to 500°.

2. If you are using shell oysters, remove the towels and place about a tablespoon of the barbecue sauce on each oyster and place in the oven. The oysters will stand up better and hold heat better if you place them on a bed of rock salt. Bake for 10 to 12 minutes. Serve immediately.

3. If you are using the jar oysters, heat a sauté pan with the olive oil in it. Dredge the oysters in the flour, shake off the excess, and quickly crisp the outside of the oysters in the oil. The oil should sizzle when the oysters hit it. Turn oysters and cook other side.

4. When the oysters have shrunk and firmed (no more than 3 or 4 minutes), deglaze with the barbecue sauce. Serve immediately. I like to present them in onion soup bowls.

Antoine's restaurant in New Orleans—where this dish was conceived in 1899 by Jules Alciatore— will not divulge its recipe for this dish of baked oysters. The dish originated, so the story goes, as an attempt to replace snails, which were in short supply. Jules gave the name "Rockefeller" to the dish because it was so rich. Every proprietor of Antoine's since Jules has made the same claim; to wit, there is no spinach in the dish. Whatever. They do use a purée of some type of "greens."

So how does my Rockefeller differ from the traditional version, other than the use of a few fresh herbs not normally found in the dish? I do not purée the mixture. I prefer it "chunky" where I can see and feel the individual ingredients. Also, I cook it at a very high temperature for a shorter period of time. Many folks have found they like my way.

| INGREDIENT | QUANTITY |
|---|---|
| Oysters | 3 dozen |
| Bacon, finely minced | 1 lb. |
| Butter, unsalted | ¼ lb. |
| Green onions, minced | 2 bunches |
| Spinach, cooked, drained, and minced | 3 c. |
| Parsley, minced | 1 c. |
| Celery, finely minced | 2 c. |
| Garlic, minced | 3 tbsp. |
| Cilantro, minced | 2 tbsp. |
| Anise, fresh if available, minced | 3 tbsp. |
| Basil, fresh, minced | ½ c. |
| Herbsaint | ½ c. |
| Tabasco | To taste |
| Worcestershire | 1 tsp. |
| Salt | To taste |
| Pepper, black, freshly ground | To taste |
| Bread crumbs | 1 c. |

**METHOD**

1. Shuck oysters (see pages 50–51).
2. Sauté bacon until browned and crisp. Drain.
3. Melt ½ stick of butter and sauté all vegetables for 4 or 5 minutes.
4. Deglaze with the Herbsaint.
5. Add Tabasco, Worcestershire, salt, and pepper.
6. Either cool before finishing dish or immediately top the oysters and bake. (This is very important. Never mix hot and cold food and allow them to stand for any period of time.)
7. Place approximately 1 tablespoon of the purée on top of each oyster and dot with remaining butter. Place oysters on a bed of rock salt in a shallow baking pan.
8. Bake in a 500° oven for about 10 minutes or until top is lightly browned.

# *poached louisiana oysters "rockefeller"*

Chef Anne Kearney at Peristyle has a philosophy of food that includes, as she told me, paying "respect to the classic dishes and flavor profiles of Louisiana. I reinterpret the classics (ingredients, origin, etc.) and the results are my version."

Her recipes are quite detailed, leaving no room for confusion. I like that. I am going to leave nearly all her comments and instructions in her recipes. I am impressed both by her absolute adherence to classical technique and by the creativity she displays while paying homage to the Creole tradition.

Although the following recipe (pages 55–57) has several parts, I do not think it beyond the home cook. I would not lose any sleep, however, if I did not have the fish bones for the fumet at hand. Anne's fumet comes about as a result of fish butchering in the normal course of events in the professional kitchen. We try to throw nothing away. Anne describes herself, self-effacingly, as "The Queen of Utilization." Chicken stock would probably suffice.

Robert Mondavi gave the portrait seen in the second photospread of this book to Anne when she won the Robert Mondavi Culinary Award of Excellence in 1998. Since 1995, this award has been given annually to just a handful of chefs. The portraitist, Rise Delmar Ochsner, has painted the chefs for this prestigious prize for several years now. (Susan Spicer was one of the winners in the inaugural year of the awards.)

To earn the award, the chefs must 1. enjoy a reputation for consistent excellence in cuisine; 2. exhibit an innovative approach to food preparation; 3. emphasize fresh, seasonal ingredients; 4. highlight authentic ethnic or regional cuisine; and 5. appreciate that wine is an integral part of cuisine and, with that appreciation, prepare menus that pair well with wines from a carefully chosen wine list.

Ms. Ochsner has painted dozens of the best chefs in the country. Of all her portraits I have seen, I think the one of Anne in this book is among the very best. Although she now resides in Santa Barbara, California, Ms. Ochsner lived for many years in New Orleans. While there, she painted a group portrait of several New Orleans chefs. Chef Anne Kearney's mentor, John Neal, was among them.

# oysters: peristyle "rockefeller"

Plump bayou oysters, baby spinach, tender fennel, leeks and onions gently poached in a rich pastis-infused velouté finished with organic Mt. Tam cheese and apple-wood-smoked bacon. And here is the recipe for your kitchen at home. This will feed 8.

**LAGNIAPPE** - Here is a little glimpse inside the professional kitchen. This is the recipe as it looks when handed to the sauté cook in her kitchen:

1. Medium dice of fennel stem (⅙), red onion (⅙), leeks (⅙), and celery (⅙), cooked in butter until just tender; season with salt and pepper, no color.
2. Velouté, made with whitefish fumet, thickened with beurre manié as needed.
3. Flamed pastis held in a squirt bottle.
4. Whole spinach leaves, baby.
5. Fresh oysters, 6 to 8, depending on the size.
6. Mt. Tam triple cream cheese made by Cowgirl Creamery (peel the crust off with a peeler and cut into ½-inch pieces), added toward the end. Adjust seasoning, then add a medium dice of rendered apple-wood-smoked bacon.
7. Plate up in the oyster dish and garnish with toasted croutons cut to mirror the same size as the rendered bacon pieces.

## INGREDIENT / QUANTITY

| INGREDIENT | QUANTITY |
|---|---|
| Butter, unsalted | 2 tbsp. |
| Medium dice red onion | ½ c. |
| Medium dice leek (whites) | ½ c. |
| Medium dice fennel | ½ c. |
| Medium dice celery | ½ c. |
| Thickened fumet (recipe follows) | 2 c. |
| Flamed pastis (Pernod, Ricard, or another anisette liquor will do) | ½ c. |
| (Anne flames the alcohol ahead in a pot by itself to prevent the vegetables from scorching.) | |
| Baby spinach, picked of stems, washed and dried | 2 c. |
| Medium select oysters, washed | 48–64 |
| (Anne gets her oysters from P&J Oysters on Toulouse Street. She says, "The oysters make the dish.") | |
| Mt. Tam cheese | 3 oz. |
| (This is one of her favorite artisan cheeses with a "mellow, earthy flavor.") | |
| Medium dice apple-wood-smoked bacon | 4 oz. |
| (Render slowly until it is crisp, then drain and place on paper towels for 15 minutes to absorb excess fat) | |
| Kosher salt and freshly ground white pepper | To taste |
| (At Peristyle, they grind all their spices as needed.) | |

*continued*

# fumet for the veloute

(Anne says this is a mild fumet but "does the trick" for the oysters in the dish.)

| INGREDIENT | QUANTITY |
|---|---|
| Whitefish bones | 1 lb. |
| Yellow onions, chopped | ¾ c. |
| Celery, chopped | ¼ c. |
| Beurre Manié (recipe follows) | ¼ c. |
| Garlic cloves, crushed | 1 |
| Lemon juice | ½ tsp. |
| Large bay leaf | 1 |
| White peppercorn | 6 |
| White wine | 2 c. |
| Water | 1 qt. |
| Parsley | 1 sprig |
| Thyme | 1 sprig |

## METHOD

1. Wash the bones in cold water. Drain well.

2. Place all ingredients except parsley and thyme in a large pot. Slowly bring to a boil, turn down heat to a simmer, and cook for 25 minutes.

3. Add the herbs and continue cooking for 5 more minutes.

4. Remove fish scraps with a spider (a kind of skimmer available in cookware stores) and discard. Strain liquid through a chinoise (a conical "strainer" available in cookware stores) lined with a damp kitchen towel.

5. Return the fumet to the stove in a clean pot, bring to a boil, and mount in ¼ cup beurre manié. Whisk until the beurre manié is dissolved, then simmer on low for 15 minutes. Cool in an ice bath.

6. Cover and store until needed.

## BEURRE MANIÉ:

Anne made particular note when talking to me of the fact that this is a handy alternative to the ever-present roux. This is a classic French technique for thickening—mostly lighter, white sauces. Basically, this is just an uncooked roux. Anne suggests the home cook might want to make it and keep it around for quick thickening.

| | | |
|---|---|---|
| Unsalted butter, softened (not melted) | 3 tbsp. | Place both ingredients in a small mixer bowl with the paddle attachment and mix until uniform. Chill thoroughly until needed in an airtight container. Shelf life: 7 days. |
| Flour, all-purpose | 3 tbsp. | |

> **LAGNIAPPE** - I first saw a beurre manié many years ago while watching Julia Child one day. She did it by hand. Beurre manié means "kneaded butter." As I recollect, she was making coq au vin.

## FINISHING THE DISH AND PRESENTATION

1. In a 4-quart sauce pot, melt the 2 tbsp. butter; add the onion, leek, fennel, and celery; stir to coat with the butter; and cook over medium heat until the vegetables are tender (no color please, just flavor).

2. Season the vegetables with salt and pepper. Add the velouté, pastis, and spinach and bring to a boil. Add the oysters and cheese. Stir to combine.

3. Slowly cook, stirring gently and frequently until the oysters begin to firm up (their lips will begin to curl). This will take only 4 to 8 minutes. Stir in the bacon.

4. Taste, adjust the seasonings, and divide between 8 warmed dishes (I prefer to serve them in shallow bowls or gratin dishes).

# oysters bienville

Jean Baptiste Le Moyne, Sieur de Bienville, is considered the founder of New Orleans in 1718. He accompanied Iberville on his original expedition to the mouth of the Mississippi in 1698. Bienville was governor on and off until 1743, when he left Louisiana. His name is all over New Orleans, and this baked oyster dish is without doubt the most succulent monument to his name. The Bienville Sauce here also goes quite well with grilled fish and may be used with fish baked en papillote. The dish was conceived at Arnaud's. Most versions of this dish will have you mincing the shrimp and mushrooms. I like to slice the mushrooms thinly and allow the shrimp to make a visual image as well.

| INGREDIENT | QUANTITY |
|---|---|
| Oysters, shucked | 3 dozen |
| Butter, unsalted | ½ lb. |
| Green onions, minced | 1 bunch |
| Mushrooms, thinly sliced | ½ lb. |
| Garlic, minced | 1 tbsp. |
| Shrimp, minced | ½ lb. |
| Dry white wine | ½ c. |
| Lemon juice | 2 tbsp. |
| Flour, all-purpose | ½ c. |
| Chicken or shrimp stock | 2 c. |
| Heavy cream | ½ c. |
| Salt | To taste |
| Pepper, white | To taste |
| Tabasco | To taste |

## METHOD

1. Place the shucked oysters on a bed of rock salt in a shallow baking dish.
2. Sweat the green onions, mushrooms, and garlic in ½ of the butter.
3. In a separate pan, make a roux with the remaining butter and the flour. Do not allow the roux to color.
4. Add the shrimp to the vegetables and cook until they color.
5. Deglaze the shrimp mixture with the white wine.
6. In a separate pan, make a light roux with the remaining butter and the flour. *Do not allow the roux to color.*
7. Add stock to shrimp and vegetable mixture. Heat through.
8. Thoroughly incorporate the roux in the shrimp mixture.
9. Season with salt, pepper, and Tabasco.
10. Either cover the oysters with the Bienville sauce and bake immediately or chill the sauce for later baking.
11. Sprinkle the bread crumbs on top of the oysters. You may dot with butter if you choose.
12. Bake in a 500° oven for about 10 minutes or until lightly browned on top.

# oysters carnaval

In 1967—the year I went to Vietnam—a woman named Deirdre Stanforth published a cookbook called *The New Orleans Restaurant Cookbook*. This is the first volume I know of that made an attempt to give something of an overview to the professionals cooking in New Orleans. All the previous volumes I ran across were either distinctly down home or efforts at self-promotion. It was quite good for that era. Along with all the better-known Creole restaurants, she included a long-gone restaurant named Corinne Dunbar's.

Corinne Dunbar was a Creole aristocrat who opened her home as a restaurant. The furniture was hers. There was no menu. You ate what was prepared. You rang a bell to get in the door. On St. Charles in the Garden District, it was truly a unique experience. The restaurant at Dunbar's home closed in 1956 (but it continued at another location until 1987). I have been cooking my adaptations of several recipes from this restaurant for decades. This is very close to the original.

| INGREDIENT | QUANTITY |
|---|---|
| Oysters, shucked with shells and liquid | 6–8 dozen |
| Yellow onion, medium | 1½ |
| Garlic cloves | 2 |
| Bay leaf | 1 |
| Celery | 4 ribs |
| Fresh thyme | 1 tsp. |
| Butter, clarified, unsalted | ¼ c. |
| Bread crumbs | 1¾ c. |
| Butter, softened, unsalted | 5 tbsp. |
| Bacon, cooked | ½ lb. |
| Lemon wedges | 12 |

METHOD

1. Chop oysters and drain, reserving liquid.

2. Mince onions, garlic, and celery. Sauté until lightly brown in a sauté pan in the clarified butter. Add bay leaf and thyme.

3. Add chopped oysters. Moisten 1 cup of bread crumbs with oyster liquor and add to mixture in skillet. Simmer for about 15 minutes or until oysters have stopped drawing water.

4. Add 2 tablespoons of the softened butter and cook until butter is melted.

5. Boil and scrub oyster shells and fill with oyster mixture.

6. Sprinkle with bread crumbs and dot with remaining butter. Put in a 450° oven for 10 minutes until thoroughly heated and browned on top.

7. Serve at once, garnished with crisp bacon strips and lemon wedges.

# crab cakes à la creole

Whatever other ingredients they may have, crab cakes will nearly always include bread crumbs and eggs. They are the binder. You may substitute whatever chilies you enjoy for the red bell pepper. I usually include a jalapeño or serrano.

| INGREDIENT | QUANTITY |
|---|---|
| Lump crabmeat, picked and cleaned | 1 lb. |
| Red bell pepper, large, diced | 2 |
| Onion, yellow, minced | 1 c. |
| Butter, unsalted | ½ c. |
| Bread crumbs | 1 c. |
| Egg, large | 1–2 |
| Coleman's mustard | 1 tbsp. |
| Worcestershire | 1 tbsp. |
| Red chilies, crushed | 1 tbsp. |
| Parsley, minced | ¼ c. |
| Mayonnaise | ¾ c. |
| Salt | 1 tsp. |
| Pepper, black, freshly ground | 1 tsp. |
| Butter, clarified | ½ c. |

## METHOD

1. Set crabmeat aside in a stainless bowl.

2. Sweat bell pepper and onion in the butter until soft.

3. In a separate bowl, combine bread crumbs, egg, mustard, chilies, parsley, mayonnaise, salt, and pepper.

4. Cool pepper and onion mixture and combine with all other ingredients.

5. Gently toss crab with other ingredients. Form into patties.

6. Sauté patties in clarified butter until browned on both sides.

7. Serve on a bed of the Roasted Red Pepper Coulis (see page 61)—with a little in a side dish.

**LAGNIAPPE** - Do not attempt to use canned crabmeat to make these. Buy fresh or pasteurized lump crab from the local fish store or supermarket. Make sure you pick through every bite of the crabmeat before you begin incorporating it in the dish.

# roasted red pepper coulis

| INGREDIENT | QUANTITY |
|---|---|
| Red bell peppers, large | 6 |
| Olive oil, extra virgin | 1 c. |
| Jalapeño pepper | 1 |
| Green onion, white part only, or shallots | ¼ c. |
| Garlic, minced | 1 tbsp. |
| Stock, chicken | ½ c. |
| Balsamic vinegar | 2 tbsp. |
| Salt | To taste |
| Pepper, black, freshly ground | To taste |

## METHOD

1. Roast, peel, and deseed all peppers.

2. Dice peppers and sweat briefly in oil.

3. Add onion or shallot and sweat a minute or two more.

4. Add garlic.

5 Deglaze with stock and balsamic vinegar.

6. Purée all in food processor.

Note: You may add more stock if the coulis seems too thick.

# crawfish ravioli

If you make this as an appetizer course, four ravioli per person will be just about right. The following recipe will easily serve 8.

| INGREDIENT | QUANTITY |
|---|---|
| **RAVIOLI FILLING** | |
| Butter | ½ lb. |
| Flour | ¼ lb. |
| Onion, minced | ½ c. |
| Bay leaves | 2 |
| Green onions, minced | ½ c. |
| Cloves | 2 |
| Salt & white pepper | To taste |
| Half-and-half | 16 oz. |
| Crawfish tail meat, cooked and minced | ½ lb. |
| Brandy | 1 tbsp. |

**METHOD**

1. Make a roux with the butter and flour. Cook, stirring constantly, for 2 minutes.

2. Add onions, bay leaves, cloves, and milk. Stir, bring to a full boil. Sauce should be very thick.

3. Remove from heat and add remaining ingredients. Cool.

4. Remove cloves.

5. Make pasta dough and allow dough to rest 30 minutes. Roll into sheets and make ravioli (see procedure pages 64–65) placing about 1½ tsp. of filling for each ravioli.

6. Serve with Tomato Basil Sauce (see recipe page 63).

# tomato basil sauce

| INGREDIENT | QUANTITY | METHOD |
|---|---|---|
| Olive oil | ½ c. | 1. Sweat vegetables in olive oil with herbs. |
| Fresh basil, minced | 2 tbsp. | 2. Add remaining ingredients. |
| Garlic, minced | 1 tbsp. | 3. Simmer slowly for about 1 hour. Strain out solids. Keep warm. |
| Fresh thyme | 1 tsp. | |
| Onion, minced | 1 c. | |
| Bay leaves | 2 | |
| Carrots, minced | 1 c. | |
| Parsley, minced | ½ c. | |
| Italian tomatoes | 6 c. | |
| Tomato puree | ½ c. | |
| Dry white wine | 1 c. | |

# pasta all'uovo

This is the fresh egg pasta of Northern Italy. Notice the "all-purpose" flour. For fresh pasta you will not need any kind of "special" flour. If you could find an Italian "oo" flour that would be dandy. If not, all-purpose will be dandy, too. You will require a hand-cranked pasta machine to make the ravioli. They are quite inexpensive and handy to have around.

| INGREDIENT | QUANTITY | METHOD |
|---|---|---|
| Flour, unbleached, all-purpose | 4 c. | 1. Place flour and salt in mixer with dough hook. |
| Eggs, large | 4 | 2. Add eggs, one at a time, while mixing on slow speed. |
| Olive oil, extra virgin | 4 tbsp. | 3. Add olive oil in a stream. |
| Salt | 1 tsp. | 4. Add a little water only if the dough seems too dry. |
| Water | As needed | 5. Wrap the dough in plastic wrap and keep the dough tightly wrapped unless you are making noodles immediately. |

## MAKING THE RAVIOLI

There are several ways to approach this and none of them is "wrong." The two principal manners are either with a ravioli form and a rolling pin or by hand, cutting them with a ravioli wheel.

## WITH THE RAVIOLI FORM

1. To make the ravioli using the form: Roll the dough through the pasta machine to the finest setting and cut into 12 16-inch lengths about 6 inches wide.

2. Place one piece of the dough over the bottom section of the ravioli form, making sure that the dough overlaps all the edges of the form a little.

3. Use the top part of the form to make slight impressions in this piece of dough.

4. Put about 1½ teaspoons of filling in each impression. Dab a little water on the raised portions.

5. Cover with the other piece of dough and firmly roll over the form with a rolling pin.

6. Trim away the excess dough from around the form.

7. Knock the ravioli out through the holes in the form and place them in a single layer on a floured sheet pan.

## BY HAND

1. As before, roll each piece of dough through a pasta machine to the finest setting and cut the pieces to size.

2. Place 1½ teaspoons the filling a couple of inches apart on one piece of the dough. Dab with water between the filling and cover with the other piece of dough.

3. Press down around the mounds of filling to seal the dough—pushing all the air pockets out of the ravioli.

4. Cut in ravioli squares with a ravioli wheel. Or you may cut into rounds with a cookie cutter.

5. Place the ravioli in a single layer on a floured sheet pan.

6. Cook ravioli in boiling salted water for about 3 or 4 minutes each. Drain and serve with Tomato Basil Sauce (see page 63).

# *marinated anchovies with basil bruschetta and stewed vidalia onions*

On pages 66–70 are four unique and quite tasty starter courses from Lilette's Chef John Harris. I think all four of these are well within the ability of the serious home cook and will be time well spent and abundantly rewarded. Thanks, John. Serves 4 to 6.

| INGREDIENT | QUANTITY |
|---|---|
| Marinated Spanish anchovies | ¾ lb. |
| Julienned Vidalia onions | 6 c. |
| Extra virgin olive oil | 3½ c. |
| Baguettes | 2 |
| Fresh basil | 6 oz. |
| Garlic cloves, smashed | 8 |

## METHOD

1. To prepare the stewed onions, put 2 cups extra virgin olive oil and 4 cups of julienned onions in small saucepot. Bring to a boil, reduce heat, and simmer for 20 minutes.

2. Add 5 smashed garlic cloves and simmer an additional 20 minutes. Season with Kosher salt and fresh cracked black pepper. Let cool.

> **LAGNIAPPE** - Olive oil should be about halfway up the onions in the pot. After simmering the liquid will cover the onions.

3. To make the basil purée, pick basil leaves (rinse & pat dry). Place in blender with 3½ cups extra virgin olive oil and 1 garlic clove. Pulse until blended but still bright green. (Color will dull if blended too long.)

4. To serve: Slice baguette on bias into long croutons. Spread liberally with basil purée and grill for 2 minutes on each side. Place two slices on a plate. Scoop 2 tablespoons of room temperature stewed onions onto each slice of baguette. Arrange 6 anchovies (3 on each slice) and garnish with fresh cracked pepper.

# eggplant crisps with skordalia and oven-dried tomatoes

Serves 4 to 6. Skordalia is a Greek "garlic sauce." Chef Harris's version is mild relative to the skordalia you will find in Greece.

## INGREDIENTS | QUANTITY

### EGGPLANT CRISPS

| Ingredient | Quantity |
|---|---|
| Firm eggplant (although any type of eggplant is usable) | 1 large |
| Whole milk | 1 qt. |
| Egg whites | 6 |
| Bread crumbs, unseasoned | 4 c. |
| Vegetable oil | 4 c. |

### SKORDALIA

| Ingredient | Quantity |
|---|---|
| Idaho potato | 1 large |
| Heavy cream | 2–3 oz. |
| Butter, unsalted | 2 oz. |
| Sour cream | 1 tbsp. |
| Lemon juice | 1 tbsp. |
| Almonds, sliced | 1 c. |
| Garlic, roasted | 1 head |
| Garlic, chopped | 1 clove |
| Olive oil, extra virgin | To taste |
| Kosher salt and cracked black pepper | To taste |

## METHOD

### EGGPLANT CRISPS

1. Peel the eggplant and slice in ¼-inch rounds.

2. Soak in milk for 1 hour (removes bitterness and helps with crispness).

3. Whip egg whites until frothy.

4. Dredge in whites and then bread crumbs (may be held for several hours).

5. Heat vegetable oil to 350° in a deep, wide thick-bottom pot.

### SKORDALIA

1. Peel and dice potato; cover in cold, salted water. Simmer until fork tender. On the side, heat the heavy cream, butter, and sour cream. Rice the potatoes into the cream mixture, season, and adjust consistency.

2. Toast almonds for 10 minutes in a 350° oven or until golden brown. Pulse in a Cuisinart until fine but not a paste. Add the potato mixture. Add the rest of the ingredients except for some of the lemon juice for adjustment later. Season and hold.

continued

## OVEN-DRIED ROMA TOMATOES

| | |
|---|---|
| Ripe Roma tomatoes (cored, halved lengthwise, and seeds removed) | 6 |
| Garlic, chopped | 1 tsp. |
| Thyme, fresh, chopped | 1 tsp. |
| Salt and pepper | To taste |
| Olive oil, extra virgin | ¼ c. |
| Basil leaves, picked, fresh | 1 c. |
| Oil-cured black olives in herbs de Provence | 1 c. |

## OVEN-DRIED ROMA TOMATOES

1. Preheat oven to 250°.

2. Toss seeded Roma tomatoes with the thyme, garlic, salt, pepper, and olive oil.

3. On a cookie pan or sheet tray lined with parchment, lay tomatoes cut side down and place in oven for about an hour, then turn them over and continue baking until most of the moisture has dissipated. Let cool slightly and peel skin while warm. These tomatoes can be done up to 2 days in advance.

## TO SERVE

1. Fry eggplant for about 2 to 3 minutes each side. Remove from oil and pat dry on paper towels. Season with salt and pepper.

2. Layer eggplant with skordalia, basil, and tomato, then repeat and place one slice of eggplant on top.

3. Plate with skordalia on the bottom to steady the eggplant. Garnish the plate with oil-cured olives and serve.

**LAGNIAPPE -** Herbs de Provence is most often a blend of dried marjoram, thyme, summer savory, basil, rosemary, fennel seeds, and lavender and is found in the cooking of southern France. Sold as a proprietary spice mixture, it may be purchased at specialty foods stores and some supermarkets.

# grilled beets with goat's cheese and walnuts

Try Laura Chenel's goat cheese with this dish—or one from the Cowgirl Creamery. Makes 4–6 servings.

| INGREDIENT | QUANTITY |
|---|---|
| Beets, large whole | 6 |
| Goat cheese (soft) | ½ lb. |
| Walnuts | 1¼ c. |
| Chives (cut into matchsticks) | ¼ c. |
| Butter | ½ stick |

## MARINADE

| | |
|---|---|
| Salt | ¼ tsp. |
| Pepper, black | ¼ tsp. |
| Thyme leaves, dry | ¼ tsp. |
| Paprika | ¼ tsp. |
| Basil leaves, dry | ¼ tsp. |
| Oregano, dry | ¼ tsp. |
| Onion powder | ¼ tsp. |
| Garlic powder | ¼ tsp. |
| Vegetable oil | ¾ c. |
| Cayenne pepper | Pinch |

## VINAIGRETTE

| | |
|---|---|
| Red wine vinegar | 1½ oz. |
| Pomace olive oil | 2 oz. |
| Walnut oil | 1 oz. |
| Salt and pepper | To taste |

## PREPARATION INSTRUCTIONS FOR GRILLED BEETS

1. Cover beets by 3 inches with cold water in a large sauce pot. Bring water to a boil and simmer until paring knife slides out of beet when pricked. Strain and let cool.

2. While running under water, rub beets with towel to remove skin. Slice beets into ½-inch rounds.

3. Prepare marinade by combining all dry ingredients in large bowl. Mix well and add vegetable oil. Toss sliced beets and hold.

4. To prepare the walnuts, melt butter in a 10-inch skillet and add walnuts. Cook, stirring occasionally, for 5 minutes and season well with salt and pepper. Reserve leftover butter.

5. For the vinaigrette, add all ingredients and the walnut butter. Whisk well.

6. To finish, grill beets on both sides for 2 minutes and toss in vinaigrette. Place 4 to 6 slices of beets on each plate and drizzle with vinaigrette.

7. Add 5 dollops of goat cheese (1 to 2 oz.) per serving, sprinkled with walnuts, and chives.

# duck confit with savoy spinach and mushroom vinaigrette

You may be able to find the Muscovy duck. But, if not, the dish will still be quite good with the Pekin duck in your local supermarket. Serves 10.

| INGREDIENT | QUANTITY |
|---|---|
| Rendered duck fat | 1 gal. |
| Muscovy duck legs | 12 |
| Kosher salt | 1 c. |
| Herbs de Provence | ¼ c. |
| Savoy spinach | 1 lb. |
| Assorted mushrooms (cremini, oyster, shiitake) | 3 lb. |
| White balsamic vinegar | ⅓ cup |
| Sherry vinegar | ⅓ cup |
| Thyme, fresh, chopped | 1 tbsp. |
| Garlic, chopped | 1 tbsp. |
| Olive oil, extra virgin | 1 cup |
| Dijon mustard | 1 tbsp. |

## METHOD

1. Cure duck legs by mixing together kosher salt and Herbs de Provence. Sprinkle on both sides of duck liberally (confit should be salty). Let sit for 24 hours.

2. Melt duck fat into a casserole that will accommodate 12 duck legs in one layer. Submerge duck legs. Fat must cover duck legs completely.

3. Place in 300° oven for about 2½ hours until thigh bone is easily removed. Ducks may be held in fat for up to one month.

4. Sauté all mushrooms (separately) in vegetable oil. Season well. Cool and chop finely.

5. Put mushrooms in a bowl. Add all remaining ingredients. The vinaigrette should be broken (not emulsified). Remember: All vinaigrette recipes are not set in stone. Adjust vinegar and oil amounts if necessary.

## TO SERVE

Pull duck legs from fat and crisp in a nonstick pan. Heat through in oven. Toss spinach with the mushroom vinaigrette and serve confit on top.

**LAGNIAPPE** - Check your local specialty food store for the rendered duck fat. If you have no luck there, there are many vendors on the Internet. Try not to let the price render *you* speechless.

# muffuletta

The origin of this king of sandwiches is attributed to the Central Grocery in New Orleans. It dates from around 1910, when Salvatore Lupa began making it for hungry farmers who came into the market. There are multitudinous versions of it now in New Orleans. Here is my favorite. *The Commercial Appeal* newspaper in Memphis chose several years ago to run my muffuletta as opposed to any of the well-known versions in New Orleans.

| INGREDIENT | QUANTITY |
|---|---|
| Round Italian loaf | 8 in. |
| Genoa salami, thinly sliced | 1 oz. |
| Provolone, thinly sliced | 1 oz. |
| Mortadella, thinly sliced | 1 oz. |
| Smoked ham, thinly sliced | 1 oz. |
| Mozzarella, thinly sliced | 1 oz. |
| Olive dressing | 2 oz. |

### METHOD

1. Slice the bread in half crosswise about 1 inch from the bottom.

2. Remove about ½ inch of the bread from inside the top and bottom of the loaf.

3. Fold over the salami, provolone, mortadella, ham, and mozzarella and layer them in the middle of the sandwich.

4. Add the olive dressing to the top of the sandwich and place the top of the loaf on all the other ingredients.

5. Slice into quarters and serve.

LAGNIAPPE - The bread is a very important ingredient in this sandwich, as is the following olive dressing. You may also add some coppa, Italian smoked pork shoulder, to the sandwich if you like. A more lavish version might include prosciutto.

# *olive dressing*

There are three basic types of olive dressing—green olive, black olive, and a combination of the two. Marinated oil or brine-cured European olives are best. If at all possible, I avoid using the canned American black olives. The brine-cured olives are what give the dressing its character. If you have a good bakery in your area, go ahead and purchase a roll or two from them to make the sandwich. If not, try the following recipe. The following Italian Roll recipe will yield 6 to 8 rolls.

| INGREDIENT | QUANTITY |
|---|---|
| Mixed Greek or Italian olives, diced | 12 oz. |
| Spanish green olives with pimentos, diced | 12 oz. |
| Pickled pearl onions, diced | 6 oz. |
| Giardiniera, diced | 6 oz. |
| Basil, dried | 1 tsp. |
| Oregano, dried | 1 tsp. |
| Garlic, minced | 1 tbsp. |
| Olive oil, extra virgin | ¼ c. |
| Balsamic vinegar | 3 tbsp. |

## METHOD

1. Mix all ingredients. Place in a nonreactive container (stainless or glass) and permit to stand a few hours in the refrigerator.

## ASSEMBLY

Slice the loaf in half cross sectionally—about an inch from the bottom. You may, if you choose, hollow out the top and bottom sections. We prefer not to. Fold the thinly sliced meats and cheeses in half. Alternately layer the meats and cheeses on the bottom section of the loaf. Place the olive dressing on the top half of the loaf and carefully put the two halves together. Slice into four wedges.

This is a *very* filling sandwich. I serve ¼ of it with the Haricot Rouge (see page 165.) It is also one of the few recipes that is easy to increase by just doubling or tripling the number of ounces in the meats and cheeses.

# italian roll for muffuletta

| INGREDIENT | QUANTITY |
|---|---|
| Warm skim milk, scalded and cooled to about 125° | 2½ c. |
| Yeast, dry | 2½ tbsp. |
| Sugar, granulated | ¼ c. |
| Flour, bread or all-purpose | 7–8 c. |
| Salt | 2 tsp. |
| Olive oil, extra virgin | ½ c. |
| Egg, large | 2 |

## METHOD

1. Combine milk, yeast, and sugar in mixer and permit to "work" for a few minutes.

2. Begin adding flour—a cup at a time. Add salt, a little at a time, as you add the flour.

3. Add olive oil in a stream.

4. Add eggs one at a time.

5. Add flour as needed until a bread-dough consistency is reached.

6. Allow rising in an oiled bowl covered with plastic wrap until double in size. Punch down.

7. Divide dough into eight equal-size pieces. Shape into balls.

8. Press or roll each ball into an 8-inch round.

9. Wash each with a little olive oil.

10. Place dough on sheet pans and allow to double again. Bake for about 15 to 20 minutes in a 425° oven.

**LAGNIAPPE** - You may sprinkle the rolls with sesame seeds if you like them. You may also add a little malt syrup to the dough. A little steam in the oven would not hurt.

# la médiatrice

The name "La Médiatrice" ("the female mediator") was apparently coined by 19th-century New Orleans husbands as a name for this useful and delectable dish. I first saw this usage in the *Picayune Creole Cookbook*. The gentlemen, arriving home at various hours, in varying states of sobriety, did not wish to appear on the stoop empty-handed to face the wrath of an irate spouse. A stop on the way was mandated to pick up this oyster loaf. Today there are many variations of this dish, now usually called a "po'boy." You may make the dish with small individual loaves of French or Italian bread or an entire baguette. In my newer version, I like to serve it, untraditionally, open-faced. You may either use the oysters in a jar or choose to shuck your own.

| INGREDIENT | QUANTITY |
|---|---|
| French bread, 2 baguettes or individual loaves | 6–8 |
| Oysters, shucked | 24–36 |
| Pernod or Herbsaint | ¼ c. |
| Salt | 1 tsp. |
| Pepper, black, freshly ground | 1 tsp. |
| Pepper, cayenne | ½ tsp. |
| Cumin, ground | ½ tsp. |
| Cornmeal, yellow | 1½ c. |
| Flour, all-purpose | 1 c. |
| Eggs, large, beaten | 3 or 4 |
| Peanut oil | 1–2 qt. |
| Aioli (see recipe, page 75) | 1 c. |
| Romaine lettuce, shredded | 2 c. |

**METHOD**

1. Using a bread knife, slice the loaf (loaves) length wise about ⅔ of the way up the side of the loaf. Use your fingers to hollow out the bottom section.
2. Marinate the oysters in the Herbsaint for an hour or so.
3. Combine in a bowl the salt, peppers, cumin, and cornmeal.
4. Dry the oysters thoroughly.
5. Dredge the oysters in the flour, then the egg, then the cornmeal.
6. Heat the peanut oil to 350°.
7. Toast the bottom of the loaf (loaves) in a hot oven.
8. Slather (I just love slathering!) the Aioli all along the inside of the toasted loaf.
9. Arrange the lettuce down inside the loaf.
10. Fry the oysters until golden brown. Drain.
11. Arrange the oysters on the bed of lettuce.

**LAGNIAPPE** - I like to serve the sandwich with lemon wedges and Tabasco sauce. You may also "dress" the sandwich with sliced tomatoes and kosher pickles.

# aioli

In the south of France, this cold sauce is most often made with raw garlic. I have found that the taste is immeasurably improved by sweating the garlic briefly in a little butter or oil. In Provence, this sauce is used with seafood, with vegetables, in soups, and as a bread spread. In New Orleans, we use it on the Médiatrice (see page 74).

| INGREDIENT | QUANTITY | METHOD |
|---|---|---|
| Garlic, finely minced | 2 tbsp. | 1. Sweat garlic in clarified butter over medium heat until soft. |
| Butter, clarified | 1 tbsp. | |
| Pepper, white, finely ground | ½ tsp. | 2. Add peppers, salt, and lemon juice. Cool slightly. |
| Pepper, cayenne | ¼ tsp. | 3. Place eggs in food processor or blender and pulse to beat. |
| Salt | ½ tsp. | |
| Lemon juice | 1 lemon | 4. Add garlic mixture to processor and pulse a few times. |
| Eggs, large | 2 | |
| Peanut oil | 2 c. | 5. While processor is running, slowly add oils in a stream. When the proper mayonnaise-like consistency has been reached, remove from processor and chill until needed. |
| Olive oil, extra virgin | ½ c. | |

**LAGNIAPPE** - Since you will require only about a cup for the Médiatrice loaf above, keep the remainder in the refrigerator to use on sandwiches, in salads, and so on. It should remain fresh and wholesome for about a week.

# rémoulade sauce

To make his rémoulade, the noted French chef Escoffier merely added chopped gherkins, capers, spices, and anchovies to a previously made mayonnaise. This produces a sauce rather more like what we now call tartar sauce than the unique emulsion we are going to make here. The following recipe is my version of one of the two basic types of rémoulade made in New Orleans. The other style is made with hard-cooked eggs, and I am not, I must confess, overly fond of it. I have an example of a third on page 78 too. Again, you will notice, we are employing whole eggs. A classic mayonnaise is made with just the yolks and olive oil. The mayonnaise I make here is lighter and lends itself better to the uses of rémoulade.

| INGREDIENT | QUANTITY |
|---|---|
| Eggs, large, whole | 3 |
| Lemon juice | 2 tbsp. |
| Red wine vinegar | 2 tbsp. |
| Salt | To taste |
| Pepper, white | To taste |
| Tabasco | To taste |
| Worcestershire | 5–6 drops |
| Garlic, finely minced | 1 tsp. |
| Horseradish, grated | 1 tsp. |
| Creole mustard | 3 tbsp. |
| Paprika | 1–2 tbsp. |
| Peanut oil | 2–3 c. |
| Parsley, finely minced | ¼ c. |
| Green onions, finely minced | ¼ c. |

**METHOD**

1. Place eggs, lemon juice, vinegar, salt, pepper, Tabasco, and Worcestershire in a food processor or blender. Pulse until smooth.

2. Add garlic and horseradish. Pulse again for a few seconds. Add mustard and paprika.

3. Add peanut oil slowly in a stream until a mayonnaise-like consistency has been reached.

4. Using a rubber scraper, remove sauce from processor and place in a stainless or glass mixing bowl.

5. Incorporate parsley and green onions. Chill immediately.

A vendor at the Crescent City Farmer's Market thoughtfully pre-packages the greens for the gumbo z'herbes.

These shrimp looked to be about a 21–25 per pound count—a good size for most of the dishes in *Creole Nouvelle*.

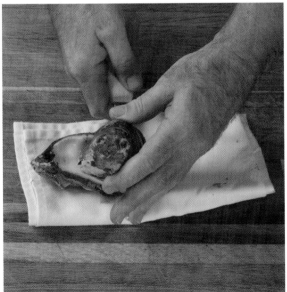

Oyster shucking does not require strength, just good technique. Follow the photos and the steps listed on pages 50–51.

Notice how you can see the various ingredients in my version of this classic from *Antoine's*.

My Muffuletta is a little taller than the original from the Central Grocery.

This may well be the single most popular appetizer in the Creole cooking classes I teach.

The tart balsamic vinegar nicely sets off the sweetness of the scallops in this modern Creole dish.

More like a stir-fry than the traditional paella-like consistency, my Jambalaya emphasizes the freshness of the seafood and vegetables.

# shrimp rémoulade

| INGREDIENT | QUANTITY |
|---|---|
| Court-bouillon (see page 13) | Several quarts |
| Gulf shrimp, unpeeled, 21–25s or 16–20s | 2 lb. |
| Romaine, shredded (chiffonade) | 1 head |
| Lemons (wedges or crowns) | 2–3 |
| Cured olives, kalamata, or Niçoise | 12–16 |
| Parsley, minced | ½ bunch |
| Paprika | Sprinkle |

## METHOD

1. Bring the court-bouillon to a boil, reduce to a simmer, and simmer for about 15 minutes.

2. Bring the heat back up to a rolling boil. Add shrimp.

3. Boil shrimp for 2 to 3 minutes. When they are pink, they are *nearly* done. Feel one. When it is no longer "spongy" and it has a firm texture, it is done.

4. Chill shrimp immediately under cold running water in a colander—add ice to aid in the chilling. (If you do not observe this step, the shrimp may still over-cook from the residual heat.)

5. Peel and devein the shrimp—do not remove the last tail joint. (The tails not only add to presentation but also provide a convenient handle for picking the shrimp up. Even the more dainty among you may find yourself in a situation where one's fingers are the best tool.)

6. Arrange the shredded romaine on a platter or individual plates. Carefully shingle the shrimp around the romaine—tails all pointing out in the same direction.

7. Finish the garnishing with the lemons, pitted olives, parsley, and paprika.

**LAGNIAPPE** - In most places in the country, you will have difficulty finding fresh shrimp. Frozen shrimp come in many different forms. I have tried nearly all of them. If you buy frozen shrimp, buy the "block-frozen" green, headless, Gulf shrimp. They are sold in sizes: 21 to 25 means there will be between 21 and 25 shrimp per pound; 16 to 20 means 16 to 20 shrimp per pound. As a rule, these shrimp are an excellent product, and the shrimp do not suffer badly if frozen in this manner.

# tujague's rémoulade sauce

As I mentioned above, there is another style of rémoulade made in New Orleans, one that is not an egg emulsion. Tujague's version is actually a third variation of rémoulade, which you will notice is really a kind of vinaigrette.

| INGREDIENT | QUANTITY | METHOD |
|---|---|---|
| White onions, finely chopped | 3 c. | Mix all chopped vegetables together. Add Creole mustard. Mix well. Add paprika, then olive oil, salt, and pepper to taste. Add a little lemon juice and vinegar to taste. Makes about 2 quarts of sauce. Sauce can be made in advance and keeps very well for quite a while. |
| Celery, finely chopped | 2 c. | |
| Green onions and green tops, finely chopped | 1 c. | |
| Fresh parsley, finely chopped | 1 c. | |
| Lettuce, finely chopped | 1 c. | |
| Creole mustard | 16 oz. | |
| Horseradish | 8 oz. | |
| Olive oil | 1½ pt. | |
| Red pepper | To taste | |
| Paprika | Generous amount to get red color | |
| Salt | To taste | |
| Lemon juice | 2 lemons | |
| Vinegar | ½ c. | |

# ravigote sauce

Ravigote sauce was omnipresent in all the older Creole restaurants and it is still quite widespread today. Very much like the Rémoulade Sauce (see page 77) it is designed for use with cold seafoods, most notably, crab, and shrimp. My version here will be ample for 3 to 4 cups of crab or shrimp serving 6 to 8.

| INGREDIENT | QUANTITY |
|---|---|
| Mayonnaise (see recipe page 81) | 1 c. |
| Creole mustard | ¼ c. |
| Fresh horseradish | ¼ c. |
| Green onion, whole, minced | 1 tbsp. |
| Parsley, minced | 1 tbsp. |
| Hard-cooked egg, large, grated | 1–2 |
| Lemon juice | 1 tbsp. |
| Kosher salt | To taste |
| White pepper | To taste |
| Capers, drained | 1 tbsp. |
| Mixed lettuces, torn | 6 c. |
| Lemon wedges | 6–8 |

## METHOD

1. Combine mayonnaise, mustard, horseradish, green onion, parsley, chopped egg, lemon juice, salt, and pepper.

2. Chop ½ of the capers and add. Thoroughly mix. Place the lettuces on chilled salad plates and mix the Ravigote with your seafood of choice reserving 1 cup of the sauce.

3. Place the seafood on the lettuce beds and garnish with a dollop of the sauce on the top of each. Finish the garnish with the reserved whole capers and the lemon wedges.

# mayonnaise

This is a simple whole-egg mayonnaise (as opposed to the French egg yolk mayonnaise), which is perfect for cold sauces like the Ravigote Sauce (see page 79).

| INGREDIENT | QUANTITY |
|---|---|
| Eggs, large, whole | 3 |
| Lemon juice | 2 tbsp. |
| White vinegar | 2 tbsp. |
| Coleman's dry mustard | 1 tsp. |
| Salt | To taste |
| Pepper, white, ground | To taste |
| Peanut oil | 2–3 c. |

**METHOD**

1. Place all ingredients, except the peanut oil, in a food processor or blender. Pulse until smooth.

2. Add oil, very slowly, in a stream until the desired consistency is obtained. Refrigerate until needed.

**LAGNIAPPE -** You may make the emulsion as thick as you like depending on the use you have in mind for the sauce. This is the reason I give the above 2–3 c. variation in the amount of oil to add.

# crab and avocado salad

Here's a salad from Chef Donald Link at Herbsaint. Look for the Haas avocados in your local supermarket. They will have a thick, pebbly skin and are green when unripe. Often, this will be what is available in your local market. You may need to plan ahead a few days here. As the avocado ripens, the skin blackens, and there will be some "give" when you lightly press the fruit. This very colorful appetizer is typical of the Creole Nouvelle style in its creative use of strong contrasting colors and complementary flavors and textures.

| INGREDIENT | QUANTITY | METHOD |
|---|---|---|
| Louisiana crabmeat | 1 lb. | 1. Pick shells out of crabmeat. |
| Beets, cooked and diced | ¼ c. | 2. Mix with basil, mayonnaise, lemon juice, and olive oil. |
| Avocados | 2 | |
| Basil leaves, fresh | 4 | 3. Season with salt and pepper and set aside. |
| Mayonnaise | 2 tsp. | 4. Toss beets in sherry vinegar, olive oil, tarragon, and salt and pepper. Set aside. Mash avocado with lime juice and salt. |
| Lemon juice | 2 tsp. | |
| Olive oil, extra virgin | ¼ c. | |
| Sherry or wine vinegar | 2 tsp. | 5. Set the avocado on the plate, add beets on top, and finish with dressed crabmeat. |
| Tarragon | 1 tsp. | |
| Limes | 2 | |
| Salt and pepper | To taste | |

# poached mirliton and artichoke salad

Here's an easy make-ahead salad using two of New Orleans' favorite vegetables. Serves 6.

| INGREDIENT | QUANTITY |
|---|---|
| Mirlitons | 3 |
| Artichoke bottoms, fresh or canned (See Eggs Sardou Recipe page 138) | 6–8 |
| Red wine vinegar | ½ c. |
| Chicken stock (see page 11) | 2 c. |
| Fresh basil, minced | 1 tbsp. |
| Parsley, minced | 2 tbsp. |
| Garlic, minced | 1 tbsp. |
| Extra virgin olive oil | 1 cup |
| Roasted red bell peppers, thinly sliced | 1 or 2 |
| Mesclun or spring mix | 12 c. |

## METHOD

1. Peel and pit the mirlitons. Slice thinly. Poach mirlitons and artichokes in vinegar and stock for about 35 minutes. Drain, reserving ½ cup of the poaching liquid.

2. Chill the mirlitons and artichokes in the refrigerator.

3. Make vinaigrette with all remaining ingredients.

4. Pour vinaigrette over mirlitons and artichokes and allow to chill for several hours.

5. Drain vegetables, reserving liquid. Toss the mesclun with just enough of the vinaigrette to coat the leaves. Place on chilled salad plates.

6. Garnish with a mound of the mirlitons and artichokes in the center of the greens. Add more vinaigrette if desired.

# corn, chile, and crab fritters

I learned the original version of this dish as a southwestern-style dish. I have adapted it using fresh lump crabmeat. I think the corn and crab go together very well.

| INGREDIENT | QUANTITY |
|---|---|
| Corn, fresh | 8–10 ears |
| Eggs, beaten, large | 3 |
| Green onions, mostly whites | ⅓ c. |
| Garlic, minced | 1 tsp. |
| Cilantro, fresh, chopped | 2 tbsp. |
| Onion, yellow or red, diced | 1¼ c. |
| Serrano or jalapeño chilies, diced | 1½ tbsp. |
| Dry rub (see page 48) | 1 tbsp. |
| Flour, all-purpose | 1¼ c. |
| Yellow cornmeal | ½ c. |
| Salt | 1 tbsp. |
| Sugar | 1 tbsp. |
| Baking powder | 1½ tbsp. |
| Coriander, dried, ground | 1 tbsp. |
| Pepper, black, freshly ground | To taste |
| Fresh lump crabmeat | ½ lb. |

## METHOD

1. Cook corn in boiling, salted water for about 8 to 10 minutes. Drain and cool. Scrape corn from cob. Puree in food processor. Add eggs.

2. Place corn mixture in a stainless bowl and add green onions, garlic, cilantro, onion, and chilies.

3. In a separate bowl, combine all dry ingredients. Thoroughly combine the two mixtures. Add lump crabmeat.

4. Fry fritters in 350° peanut oil until golden brown. Drain on toweling.

Serve with cocktail sauce (see page 22) or Rémoulade Sauce (see page 76)

# CREOLE SEAFOOD DISHES

C rabs, shrimp, oysters, pompano, crawfish, redfish—these are the foods most folks think of when they think of dining in New Orleans. Seafood dominates the regional cookery of southern Louisiana. Thousands earn their living by crabbing, shrimping, fishing, and cultivating alligators, crawfish, catfish, and freshwater shrimp. Seafood is the soul and backbone of Creole cookery. I try to hit all the high spots here.

# pan-seared scallops with balsamic vinegar/ginger beurre blanc

First and foremost, avoid "bay scallops." These are the small scallops you will see at your local fish market or supermarket. Most of these sold in the United States are farm raised in China. I am not at all fond of their texture or flavor.

Sea scallops are what you want to buy and cook—big and plump. These are mostly harvested from the waters up and down the Atlantic seaboard—from Newfoundland to North Carolina. In 1997, United States sea scallops were declared "overfished." Since that time, the National Marine Fisheries Service has developed a plan to rotate areas closed off to scallop fishing to allow habitat recovery. The sea scallop has made a great recovery and can be found in some of the best new Creole dishes today.

| INGREDIENTS | QUANTITY |
|---|---|
| Sea scallops | 1 lb. |
| Flour, all-purpose | To coat |
| Salt and pepper | To taste |
| Olive oil, extra virgin | 2 tbsp. |
| Ginger, fresh peeled and minced | 2 tbsp. |
| Garlic, minced | 1 tbsp. |
| Shallots, minced | 1 tbsp. |
| Balsamic vinegar | ¼ c. |
| Orange, juiced | ½ c. |
| Lemon, juiced | ¼ c. |
| Cold, unsalted butter, cubed | 1 lb. |
| Salt and white pepper | To taste |
| Chives, minced | 2 tbsp. |

## METHOD

1. Dry the scallops and dredge them in the flour to which you have added salt and pepper. Get a sauté pan quite hot and add the olive oil.

2. Place scallops in pan. Allow scallops to brown for about 2 to 3 minutes on each side. Remove and keep warm.

3. In the same skillet, add 2 tbsp. of butter and bring up to temperature. Sweat the minced garlic and shallots. Stir in the minced ginger.

4. Deglaze with the vinegar and juices. Bring the mixture to a full boil and allow it to boil for 5 to 6 minutes or until reduced by ¾.

5. Reduce heat and begin adding butter, never allowing mixture to boil again. Add salt and pepper to taste.

6. Ladle sauce onto a warm plate and arrange scallops on it. Sprinkle minced chives on top for garnish.

7. I like to serve this with a variant on Risotto Milanese.

# pompano en papillote

Even if you are able to find pompano at your local market you will find it to be the most expensive fish in the display case. You may substitute any fish with a little flavor and texture to it. Salmon would be a good choice—or sea bass. Here is my version of a staple at Antoine's. Serves 6 to 8.

| INGREDIENT | QUANTITY |
|---|---|
| Pompano filets, 6–8 oz. each | 6–8 |
| Clarified butter | 4 oz. |
| Shallot, diced | 3 tbsp. |
| Dry white wine | 2 c. |
| Fresh lump crabmeat | 1 c. |
| Shrimp, diced | 1 c. |
| Onion, diced | 1 c. |
| Garlic, minced | 1 tsp. |
| Fresh thyme | 1 tsp. |
| Bay leaf | 1 |
| Fish (or chicken) stock | 2 c. |
| All-purpose flour | 2 tbsp. |
| Large egg yolks | 2 |
| Salt | To taste |
| Pepper, white | To taste |

## METHOD

1. Sauté fillets with shallot in 2 tbsp. butter and add 2 c. wine. Cover and simmer slowly until fillets are tender, about 5 to 8 minutes.

2. Sweat crabmeat and shrimp 2 tbsp. butter. Add onion and garlic and simmer 5 minutes.

3. Add thyme, bay leaf, and 1¾ c. fish stock, and simmer 5 minutes.

4. Melt 2 tbsp. of the butter, add in flour and make a light roux.

5. Whisk in the remaining stock.

6. Add to crabmeat mixture with wine stock drained from fillets. Simmer, stirring constantly, until thickened. Beat egg yolks and mix with sauce and remaining ¼ c. wine. Add salt and pepper to taste. Chill in refrigerator until firm.

7. Cut 6 to 8 large parchment hearts by folding the full sheet of parchment in half—use most of the paper. Draw a large half-heart on the paper and cut it out. Butter the inside of the parchment.

8. Place most of the sauce (divided into 6 to 8 portions) on one side of heart, lay fish fillet on sauce, nap the top of the fillet with remaining sauce and fold over other half of paper.

9. Seal the package by folding the curved side of the paper over about one inch and crimping it all the way around.

10. Place the packets on a sheet pan and bake in a 450° oven for about 15 minutes. If you have sealed your packets well they will have puffed.

**LAGNIAPPE** - Many years ago when I first learned this technique I was actually taken aback by watching the chef blow into the end of the heart to puff it before he put it in the oven. Of course, if just the two of you are there and you know each other really well you might try it.

# shrimp with green chile grits and tasso cream sauce

Chef Donald Link of Herbsaint - Serves 6.

| INGREDIENT | QUANTITY |
| --- | --- |
| Butter, divided | 4 tbsp. |
| Onion, diced | ½ c. |
| Celery, diced | ½ c. |
| Tasso, diced | ½ c. |
| Fresh thyme, chopped | 1 tbsp. |
| Cayenne pepper | ¾ tsp. |
| Paprika | ¾ tsp. |
| Garlic, chopped | 1 tsp. |
| Flour | 4 tbsp. |
| Shrimp stock | 1 c. |
| Heavy cream | 1 c. |
| Lemon juice | Dash |
| Hot sauce | Dash |
| Oil for frying | 2 qt. |
| Large shrimp | 2 lb. |
| Salt | 1½ tsp. |
| Black pepper | 1½ tsp. |

**METHOD**

1. Melt 2 tbsp. butter in saucepan over medium heat. Add onion, celery, tasso, thyme, cayenne, paprika, and garlic and cook until vegetables are tender.

2. Add remaining 2 tbsp. butter to pan, then add flour, and mix with vegetables. Add shrimp stock and reduce by half. Add cream and reduce again until thick sauce has formed. Finish with lemon juice and hot sauce. Set aside.

3. Cook shrimp in whatever oil or fat you desire, a few minutes on each side until almost cooked through. Ladle sauce over shrimp and simmer 5 minutes.

4. To Serve: Spoon over warm grits with roasted peppers and cheese mixed in.

# shrimp and ham jambalaya

The following recipe is *very* different from the traditional Jambalaya, which is primarily a rice dish similar to paella. Everyone who cares is pretty much in agreement that the "jamb" in "jambalaya" is derived from the French *jambon* (which comes from *jambe* or "leg") for ham. There are several notions about the origin of the rest of the word, though.

This favorite southern Louisiana hodgepodge can be made with almost any combination of meat, poultry, or seafood. The combination of meat and shellfish in the dish probably owes its origin to the Spanish influence in Louisiana, although the combination is not terribly common in Spain. My method for making this dish is not typical. I have had versions of this dish, baked, that resemble a spicy, lumpy library paste. Not only do I make it like a stir-fry, but also I usually make it in a wok and serve it *over* steamed rice. This method retains the freshness and crispness of the vegetables and seafood.

| INGREDIENT | QUANTITY | METHOD |
|---|---|---|
| Clarified butter or peanut oil | ¼ c. | 1. Heat butter or oil in a pan large enough to hold all the ingredients. |
| Onion, sliced in a thin julienne | 2 c. | |
| Bell pepper, sliced in a thin julienne | 2 c. | 2. Sauté the onion, bell pepper, and celery until just beginning to brown. |
| Celery, sliced thinly on the bias | 3–4 ribs | |
| Garlic, minced | 1 tbsp. | 3. Add shrimp and sauté just until firm and colored. |
| Shrimp, medium to large | 1½ lb. | 4. Add tomatoes, purée, and red pepper. Add cilantro. |
| Bay leaves | 3 | |
| Thyme, whole | 1 tsp. | 5. Add ham and warm through. |
| Tomatoes, peeled and seeded, chopped | 3 c. | 6. Add 2 cups of the shrimp stock and thoroughly combine all ingredients. |
| Tomato purée | ½ c. | |
| Red pepper, crushed | 1 tsp. | 7. Add salt, pepper, and Tabasco. |
| Cilantro, fresh | 1 tsp. | 8. Thoroughly mix remaining half cup of cold stock with the cornstarch and add them to the dish. Cook until the starch clears. |
| Ham, not too smoky, large julienne | ½ lb. | |
| Shrimp stock | 2½ c. | Serve over boiled or steamed rice. |
| Salt | To taste | |
| Pepper, black, freshly ground | To taste | |
| Tabasco | To taste | |
| Corn starch | 3 tbsp. | |

# shrimp creole

Like the jambalaya, I make this dish as a quick sauté. I do not believe I can stress enough how much of the flavor—in dishes where we add a liquid—comes from the stock and how *much* these dishes are improved when the vegetables, seafoods, and meats are not overcooked. The following amounts are a one-person serving because one will not always be cooking for a group. The sauté dishes—all of them—are easily prepared for one or two.

You will find the Creole Sauce in chapter 2 (page 23).

| INGREDIENT | QUANTITY | METHOD |
|---|---|---|
| Clarified butter or extra virgin olive oil | 1 oz. | 1. Heat clarified butter in a sauté or fry pan until very hot. |
| Flour | To coat | 2. Dredge shrimp in flour and shake off excess. |
| Shrimp, medium to large, peeled and deveined | 6–8 | 3. Sauté shrimp until colored and crisped, tossing the pan all the while. |
| Dry white wine | 2 oz. | 4. Deglaze with white wine. |
| Creole sauce | 6 oz. | 5. Add Creole sauce and toss until all shrimp are thoroughly coated. |
| | | 6. Serve with a rice pilaf or boiled rice. |
| | | Colored with turmeric or saffron, the pilaf makes a more dramatic presentation. |

# sole doré

This is my personal favorite sautéed fish, provided that the sole is impeccably fresh and the texture is firm. This was a popular dish during the period I was night chef at the original Scott's Seafood Grill and Bar in San Francisco (we used petrale sole there), and I have served it at many restaurants since that time. The word *doré* in French means "gilded" or "golden-colored." The piece of fish will look like an omelet when properly prepared. Serve it with the Beurre Blanc (see page 21).

A very quick dish to prepare, it should only take 3 or 4 minutes total cooking time.

**LAGNIAPPE** - America has no sole. All the fish sold as sole in this country are really varieties of flounder. No, the scales are not being pulled over your eyes. It is perfectly legit. Sole is a European fish. The fish purveyors are permitted to call these flounder sole as long as some qualifier is added—"gray" sole or "lemon" sole, for example. This makes absolutely no difference as far as the preparation of this dish is concerned.

| INGREDIENT | QUANTITY |
|---|---|
| Filet of sole, 5–6 oz. | 6–8 pieces |
| Flour, all-purpose | 1 c. |
| Pepper, white, finely ground | 1 tsp. |
| Pepper, cayenne, finely ground | 1/2 tsp. |
| Salt | 1 tsp. |
| Eggs, large, whole, beaten | 6 |
| Butter, clarified | 3–4 oz. |

**METHOD**

1. Thoroughly dry the filets and dredge them in the flour in which you have mixed the peppers and the salt.

2. Place them in the eggs in a bowl. (You may do this ahead and refrigerate the fish.)

3. Place the clarified butter over medium-high heat in a sauté pan.

4. Lift the filets from the eggs and lay them in the clarified butter.

5. Cook until golden brown on the presentation side, then turn and cook until done.

# sautéed speckled trout with beurre noisette

The speckled trout, more properly known as the spotted seatrout, is one of the principal gamefish found in the coastal marshes of Louisiana and Texas. This fish is actually not a member of the trout family. It is related to the drum. The smaller examples will fare better with the following recipe. You may also prepare true trout—rainbow, brown, lake, etc.—with this technique.

| INGREDIENT | QUANTITY |
|---|---|
| Trout, 10 oz. cleaned | 6–8 |
| Flour, seasoned | 2 c. |
| Eggs, beaten | 3–4 |
| Cornmeal | 2 c. |
| Salt | 1 tsp. |
| Pepper | To taste |
| Clarified butter | ½ c. |
| Whole butter, unsalted | 2 tbsp. |
| Lemon juice | 1 tbsp. |
| Parsley, minced | ½ c. |

**METHOD**

1. Dip trout in flour, beaten egg, then in cornmeal mixed with the salt and pepper. Heat butter in a heavy skillet, sauté fish for 4 to 5 minutes on each side.

2. Remove trout from pan to serving platter.

3. Add whole butter to skillet and cook until slightly browned. Squeeze in lemon and add parsley. Pour over trout.

# sea bass

The sea bass family encompasses a fairly large group of fish. Most of them react in the same versatile manner to cooking, though. This fish may be grilled, sautéed, baked or poached. The very short ingredient list here is typical of the flavor combinations we use with delicate-flavored (although not necessarily delicate-fleshed—this is a fairly firm fish) fish or shellfish.

| INGREDIENT | QUANTITY | METHOD |
|---|---|---|
| Sea bass, filleted, skinned and portioned, 6 oz. | 6–8 filets | 1. Dry the sea bass and dredge it in the flour. Shake off excess. |
| All-purpose flour | 1 c. | 2. Heat the butter or olive oil quite hot in a sauté or fry pan. |
| Clarified butter or extra virgin olive oil | 6 oz. | 3. Sear the bass on both sides and deglaze with the wine and lemon juice. |
| Dry white wine | 6–8 oz. | |
| Lemon juice | ¼ c. | 4. Place bass in a 500° oven until fish begins to flake—5 to 6 minutes. |
| Salt | To taste | 5. Add salt and pepper. |
| White pepper | To taste | |

**LAGNIAPPE -** The dish may be served with just the pan sauce or with beurre blanc (see recipe page 21) or even Hollandaise sauce (see recipe page 16).

# crawfish étouffée

The word "Étouffée" used in a culinary sense means to cook or serve in a closed vessel. It comes from the French word meaning to suffocate or smother. So these are smothered crayfish—smothered in the *Trinity*.

| INGREDIENT | QUANTITY |
|---|---|
| Butter, clarified | 12 oz. |
| Flour, all-purpose | 6 oz. |
| Onions, diced, medium dice | 1 c. |
| Celery, diced, medium dice | 4 ribs |
| Bell peppers, diced | 2 |
| Garlic, minced | 1 tsp. |
| Pepper, red, ground | 1 tsp. |
| Pepper, red, crushed | 1 tsp. |
| Pepper, black, ground | 1 tsp. |
| Pepper, white, ground | 1 tsp. |
| Cumin, ground | 1 tsp. |
| Cilantro, fresh, chopped | 1 tsp. |
| Thyme, leaf or whole | 1 tsp. |
| Salt | To taste |
| Stock, seafood or court-bouillon | 24 oz. |
| Crayfish tails | 1 lb. |
| Green onions, chopped | 1 bunch |

## METHOD

1. In a thick fry pan or sauté pan, make a medium brown roux with 6 ounces of the butter and the flour. Set aside.

2. In a separate pan, sweat the onions, celery, bells, and garlic in 3 ounces of the butter. Cook until the vegetables are just soft.

3. Place all the spices and herbs in the stock or court-bouillon in a saucepan and bring to a simmer.

4. Using a wire whip, incorporate enough of the roux into the stock to obtain a sauce-like consistency.

5. In a sauté pan, sauté crayfish in remaining butter quickly over high heat until they begin to brown. Add green onions to pan.

6. Add all the other vegetables to the crayfish mixture.

7. Add crayfish mixture to the sauce and simmer for 5 minutes. Check seasoning.

   Serve with plain boiled or steamed rice.

# crabs

It is time to get crabby, something most chefs come by naturally. But in this case we are discussing the blue crab. Before you cook them, you will need to know a little about cleaning them. Blue crabs come to market in a couple of ways—either as hard-shell crabs or soft-shell crabs. We clean each a little differently. See the photographs in the second photospread for an illustration of this process.

Unless you know someone you can trick into cleaning the crabs for you—in which case you are far more clever than I—you are going to need to know the basics of crab cleaning to make a stuffed crab dish. I have done my very best to restrict the number of labor-intensive procedures here in the book. I know. I know I have not always succeeded. Shut up.

## METHOD

1. Place the crab in front of you, shell side up. Remove the two large claws by twisting them away from the body. Set the claws aside for now.

2. The crab has two very sharp points on either side of the body. Lift the crab and, holding it with one hand, with the other hand pull up on one of the points. The top shell should lift off easily.

3. Cut off the "jaws" of the crab where they join the lower shell and remove the internal organs by scraping them out with a knife—after you have done this a few time you may use your fingers. Using your fingers, strip away the "dead-men's fingers" (gills) running down either side of the body. Throw them away. Using a sharp knife, make a straight, deep cut from the back of the crab, on both sides of the crab, just above the leg joints. Put these two pieces aside for now.

4. Using your knife again, cut off the legs where they join the body. Using your thumb or fingers, hold the back fin (shaped like a paddle) meat in place.

5. Find the large piece of white meat on either side of the body of the crab (this is called the "back fin" or "lump" meat) and remove it with your knife.

6. All the rest of the white meat in the body is located in the chambers running down either side of the crab separated by thin slats of cartilage. Remove this meat from the chambers by sliding the knife under and lifting it out. This meat is known as the "flake" meat.

7. You are almost there. Now you are ready to remove the meat from the two pieces you set aside above. The chunk of white meat on the top of the back fin will come off easily. You will now see a piece of cartilage. Cut under this and remove the rest of the meat.

8. Okay, back to the claws. Crack the claw with the back of your knife and open it. You should be able to pull the meat out easily.

9. Check all the bits of meat you now have for pieces of shell or cartilage. Throw away all the debris. Put crab meat in a bowl. Wash shell out thoroughly. You are now ready to stuff a crab.

# deviled stuffed blue crab

Most of the *older* Creole restaurants have their version of this classic dish. Here is mine. The "deviling"—and not much of it—comes from the Coleman's mustard. Unlike the older version, I use all fresh herbs and incorporate a little of the Velouté (see page 18), which makes the stuffing creamy. Serves 8.

| INGREDIENT | QUANTITY |
|---|---|
| Olive oil, extra virgin | ¼ c. |
| Onions, chopped | 1½ c. |
| Green onions, chopped | 1½ c. |
| Celery, diced | ¾ c. |
| Bell pepper, red, diced | ½ c. |
| Garlic, minced | 6 cloves |
| Parsley, fresh, minced | ½ c. |
| Thyme, fresh | 1 tbsp. |
| Sage, fresh | ½ tsp. |
| Cayenne | 1 tsp. |
| Bay leaves | 2 or 3 |
| Coleman's dry mustard | 2 tsp. |
| Bread crumbs | 1½ c. |
| Fresh ground black pepper and sea salt | To taste |
| Eggs, large | 2 |
| Lump crab meat | 16 oz. |
| Paprika | 1 tbsp. |
| Lemon juice, fresh | 1 tsp. |
| Lemon zest | 1 tbsp. |
| Dry white wine | ½ c. |
| Butter, unsalted, melted | ½ c. |
| Seafood velouté | 1 c. |

## METHOD

1. Sweat the onion, green onion, celery, and bell pepper for 3 or 4 minutes in the olive oil over medium heat.

2. Add garlic, parsley, sage, cayenne, Coleman's, bay leaves, and thyme and continue cooking over medium heat, stirring for an additional 2 or 3 minutes.

3. Remove from the heat, place in a bowl, and cool. Remove bay leaves.

4. Add the bread crumbs, eggs, crabmeat, paprika, lemon juice, and zest. Add pepper and salt. Moisten the mixture with ½ cup of wine. Combine thoroughly. Incorporate velouté.

5. Preheat the oven to 450°.

6. Stuff the clean shells. Place them in a baking dish. You may want to add a little more bread crumbs and paprika to the top of each. Drizzle a little of the butter over the crabs and bake for about 20 minutes.

# soft-shell blue crabs

In Louisiana, you will often hear these crabs referred to as "busters." Blue crabs molt every year in the spring. In other words, they "bust" out of their shells. They do this by filling themselves up with water. Of the couple of different ways of handling the crabs, both techniques have their adherents. Some like to let nature take its course, and others like to remove the shells by hand. The latter procedure usually results in the loss of legs and claws.

"Crabbers" catch these crabs in the spring just before they molt. They are then held live in tanks until they shed their shells. The crabs are graded into five sizes: medium, hotels, primes, jumbos, and whales. Many packers then pack them in wet straw and ship them all over the country live. Depending on where you live, you may find them available only as a frozen product. These are quite good, too.

The soft-shell crab consists of over 90% edible meat. They are much easier to clean than the hard-shell crab.

**LAGNIAPPE** - Antoine's and Brennan's offer soft-shell crabs on their menus. They will appear seasonally on many menus around town. If it is a permanent fixture on a menu, it is probably frozen. Depending on the size of crabs you are able to obtain, you will need to vary your portion sizes for both main courses and appetizers.

## METHOD

1. To clean a soft-shell crab cut off the "jaws" (mouth) just as you did with the hard-shell crab. Cut about ¼ inch into the shell.

2. Lift aside the soft, papery shell. Remove the "dead man's fingers" (gills) as with the hard-shell crab. Replace the shell.

3. Then remove the "apron," the bell-shaped flap from the bottom of the body, rinse the crab under cold running water, and you are ready to cook.

# beer-batter-fried soft-shell crabs

The method for this recipe is a very traditional manner in which to cook soft-shell crabs. I think my beer batter is an improvement on the batters used by many New Orleans restaurants. This batter seals in all the succulence of the crab. This recipe is for a main course–size portion. Halve it for an appetizer.

| INGREDIENT | QUANTITY |
| --- | --- |
| Beer batter (see recipe page 98) | 1 recipe |
| Peanut oil | Approx. 1 gal. |
| Flour, all-purpose | 2 c. |
| Sea salt | 1 tbsp. |
| White pepper | 2 tsp. |
| Cayenne | 2 tsp. |
| Soft-shell crabs, jumbos | 12–16 |

METHOD

1. Make the beer batter and allow it to rest for an hour.
2. Preheat peanut oil to 350°.
3. Combine flour, salt, pepper, and cayenne in a bowl.
4. Thoroughly dry the crabs, then dredge them in the flour. Shake off excess flour.
5. Fry the crabs, a few at a time, in the oil until they are golden brown. This will probably take 5 or 6 minutes.
6. Drain them on paper towels.

**LAGNIAPPE** - You may serve the crabs with either the béarnaise or beurre blanc. Garnish them with lemon twists or crowns and a sprig of fresh parsley. I like to serve the crabs on folded white linen napkins.

# beer batter

This batter is the one I choose most often for seafoods and vegetables. The yeast makes it light.

| INGREDIENT | QUANTITY |
|---|---|
| Flour, all-purpose | 2 c. |
| Salt | 1 tsp. |
| Sugar, granulated | ½ tsp. |
| Paprika | 2 tsp. |
| Beer, warm | 18 oz. |
| Yeast, dry | 1 tsp. |
| Egg yolks, large | 2 |

## METHOD

1. Sift flour, salt, sugar, and paprika together.
2. Combine beer and yeast. Allow mixture to work a few minutes until you see the yeast bubbling.
3. Add beer mixture to flour and beat until there are no lumps.
4. Thoroughly incorporate egg yolks.
5. Allow batter to rise in a warm place for an hour or so. Punch it down and add more warm beer if it has gotten too thick.

   Refrigerate covered or use.

# crawfish pie

Made very much in the manner of and incorporating the same ingredients as a traditional pot pie made with chicken or beef, this dish is definitely a citified, upscale version. "Crawfish" is a New Orleans usage for "crayfish" for those of you who do not speak "Louisiana."

| INGREDIENT | QUANTITY |
|---|---|
| Crawfish tails with fat | 2 lb. |
| Clarified butter or cooking oil | ½ c. |
| Onions, diced | 1½ c. |
| Celery, diced | 1 c. |
| Carrots, diced | 1 c. |
| Green peas | 1 c. |
| Stock, chicken or seafood, cold | 1–2 c. |
| Cornstarch | 2 tbsp. |
| Green onions, diced | ½ c. |
| Parsley, minced | ¼ c. |
| Puff pastry, frozen (thawed) 10-by-15 sheet | 1 |

## METHOD

1. Season crawfish tails with salt and pepper and set aside.

2. Sweat onions and celery in fat over medium heat until onions are clear. Add carrots and peas. Simmer a couple of minutes.

3. Add crawfish and fat.

4. Simmer 10 minutes.

5. Combine cold stock and cornstarch. Add to crawfish mixture. Cook until thick, stirring constantly.

6. Add green onions and parsley; correct seasoning with salt and pepper, then set aside to cool.

7. Place crawfish mixture in a baking dish, cover with puff pastry, and bake at 375° until pastry is puffed and nicely browned.

   Frozen puff pastry is available in most supermarkets these days. Cut the pastry to fit the dish in which you choose to bake the pie.

# *des écrevisses bouillies (crawfish boil)*

Okay, so you want to have a New Orleans party. Well, here's a party in a pot. It is no coincidence that New Orleanians have crawfish boils around Mardi Gras every year. Yes, you heard me, a crawfish boil. No, this is not the exclusive purview of our rural cousins, the Cajuns (although they do it very well). Cultivate some friends in New Orleans—you will get invited to a crawfish boil. This is most definitely a party dish and the preparations create a party ambience.

The Louisiana crawfish season runs from fall to late spring with Mardi Gras often falling smack at the height of the season. I have done many parties where I cooked 500 pounds of these little critters and they all disappeared. In answer to your next question, no, you do not have to suck the head to enjoy crawfish. But, have a few beers and who knows. . . .

All right, let's get ready to laissez le bon temps roulet!

First, you are going throw this fête outside. You will need a pot and a propane burner. You will be able to get a 36-quart pot for around $40. (Should you later decide you want to try deep-frying a turkey you will already have your apparatus for this treat.) It will be equipped with a basket in which you will boil the crawfish. The same store will sell you a propane burner. Most of the crawfish pros suggest having an ice chest on hand, in which to "finish" the crawfish—let them steam in a closed ice chest. Actually, two ice chests are even better—one to hold the vegetables after they are cooked and one for the seafood. One last comment—unless you buy your crawfish from a roadside vendor the question of "purging" should not arise. All reputable retailers and wholesalers will have already purged the crawfish for you.

Okay, you did buy them from a roadside vendor. You already have an ice chest handy I presume. Dump your crawfish in the ice chest along with about a pound of kosher salt. Fill the chest with cold water and allow them to "purge" for 30 minutes or so. Rinse thoroughly with cold running water before cooking.

Serves 8 to 10.

| INGREDIENT | QUANTITY |
| --- | --- |
| Live crawfish | 30 lb. |
| Water | 20 gal. |
| Court-bouillon recipe ingredients (see page 13) | Triple recipe |
| Onions, peeled and quartered | 4 |
| Liquid crab boil | 2 oz. |
| Tabasco | 4 oz. |
| Peanut oil | 2 oz. |
| Lemons, cut in half | 6 |
| "B"-size red or white rose potatoes | 5 lb. |
| Corn, ears, shucked and cut in half | 8–10 ears |
| Andouille sausage, cut in two-inch pieces | 3–4 lb. |

## METHOD

1. Thoroughly rinse the crawfish with cold running water. They ain't called "mudbugs" for nothing.
2. Add court-bouillon ingredients, onions, crab boil, Tabasco, peanut oil, and lemons to the pot—squeeze them into the water and then throw in the lemon carcasses.
3. Bring to a rolling boil.
4. Add potatoes to the liquid and boil for about 10 minutes.
5. Add corn to pot and boil for an additional 15 minutes.
6. Stab a cook's fork into one of the larger potatoes. If you cannot remove the potato from the pot by lifting straight up, they are done. Lift the basket out and dump its contents into one of your ice chests. Close.
7. You may add one of the proprietary crawfish boils to the pot at this point should you choose.
8. Put the basket back in the pot and add the crawfish to the pot.
9. Boil the crawfish for about 10 minutes, add the sausage and boil an additional five minutes. Remove basket and dump into your other ice chest. Close. Let the crawfish "steam" for about 10 to 15 minutes in the ice chest.
10. While the crawfish are steaming cover your tables with newspaper (I am sure this is going to be found to be unhealthy before this book is published) and/or paper grocery bags. This not only lends an authentic rustic element to your party, but aids immeasurably in the cleanup! This would also be the time to cook your crabs and shrimp if you have elected to include them.
11. Here comes the easy part of this meal. Dump your ice chests full of food right onto the paper on the tables.
12. Serve this meal with a nice crusty bread, chile sauces, Rémoulade sauce, butter for the bread, potatoes and corn, drawn butter, and lots of bibs and napkins.

**LAGNIAPPE -** If you want to have the deluxe version of this party also obtain 10 lb. of live blue crabs and 5 lb. of 16–20 gulf shrimp. You will add these to the pot after you have cooked your crawfish. They will cook in 5–6 minutes, so they will be the last things you cook. When feeding large numbers of folks I have also boiled a few sectioned chickens.

While it is difficult to pair a wine with this meal, beer provides no such worries. Pick one or two. Buy lots.

Eating crawfish: Grasp the crawfish with both hands and pull the head and tail away from each other by pulling down. Either suck the head or don't. Begin peeling the tail shell away at the top. After you have peeled a segment or two, you will be able to squeeze the meat out by pressing firmly at the bottom end of the tail. Enjoy.

# pecan encrusted catfish filets with spicy rum sauce

Yes, it is permissible to eat catfish. I still caught them in small streams myself when I was in college. I think our water was much cleaner then. Nowadays, though, with so much polluted water out there I don't know if I would still be amenable to that. Fortunately our neighbor to the east and north, Mississippi, is flush with catfish farms. Just check out the area around Belzoni, Mississippi, if you don't believe me. The farm-raised product is quite white with a clean, fresh taste and firm texture. Fried catfish just cries out for hush puppies. Can't hear it? Shhh. Hush puppies are nothing more or less than deep-fried cornbread. Serves 6 to 8.

| INGREDIENT | QUANTITY | METHOD |
|---|---|---|
| Catfish filets, 6–7 oz. | 6–8 | 1. Thoroughly dry and salt and pepper filets. |
| Kosher salt | To taste | 2. Beat the eggs and milk together. |
| Pepper, white freshly ground | To taste | 3. Dredge the filets in the seasoned flour, then in the egg mixture, and finally in the pecans. Press the pecans firmly into the fish, coating completely. |
| Eggs, large | 3 | |
| Milk | ¼ c. | |
| All-purpose flour | 1 c. | 4. Heat peanut oil to 350°. |
| Pecans, finely ground | 2 c. | 5. Fry filets until they are golden brown—about 5 to 6 minutes. Drain. |
| Peanut oil | 2 qt. | 6. Serve with Spicy Rum Sauce (see page 104). |

# chile hush puppies

Although these are served all over the South, New Orleans claims their invention. More specifically, the Ursuline nuns who came over from France created them. In the first quarter of the 18th century they were making what they called croquettes de maize. The name hush puppy came later and was attributed variously to a Creole cook and a cook in Atlanta. They were supposedly tossed to whining puppies to pacify them. I'm sure if you are from the South that you have a story, too. But, this is mine and I'm sticking to it.

These are meant to accompany the Pecan Encrusted Catfish. Serves 6 to 8.

| INGREDIENT | QUANTITY | METHOD |
|---|---|---|
| Corn meal, yellow | 1½ c. | 1. Heat peanut oil to 350°. Mix all dry ingredients. |
| All-purpose flour | ½ c. | 2. Add onion, jalapeño, and corn. |
| Baking powder | 1 tsp. | 3. Add buttermilk. You may need a little more or less than the recipe calls for. You are looking for a thick batter-like consistency, not a "dough." |
| Kosher salt | 1 tsp. | |
| Granulated sugar | 1 tsp. | |
| Onion, minced | ¾ c. | 4. Using a tablespoon-sized spoon, drop dollops of the batter into the oil. When they float and are golden brown they are cooked. Drain and serve with fried catfish. |
| Jalapeño, minced | 1–2 | |
| Fresh corn, cooked | 1½ c. | |
| Buttermilk | ½–¾ c. | |
| Peanut oil | 2 qt. | |

# spicy rum sauce

| INGREDIENT | QUANTITY |
|---|---|
| Medium red bell pepper, diced | 1 |
| Medium yellow onion, diced | 1 |
| Jalapeño or serrano pepper, minced | 1 or 2 |
| Garlic, minced | 2 tsp. |
| Fresh pineapple, diced | 2 c. |
| Dark rum | ¾ c. |
| Dark brown sugar | ¾ c. |
| Balsamic vinegar | ¼ c. |

**METHOD**

1. In a non-reactive pan bring all ingredients to a boil.

2. Reduce to a simmer and cook for about 15 minutes. Sauce should have thickened and all solids should be soft.

## MEATS AND POULTRY

In this chapter, I highlight a few of the more innovative dishes as well as some classic Creole ones. In 1981, when I opened Mudd's in San Ramon, California, for Virginia Mudd, she enjoined me not to make certain dishes. Among them was quail since she and her husband, Palmer Madden, had a number of them on their property. I made many other game and poultry dishes, such as partridge, pheasant, and poussin, usually as weekend specials.

Mudd's was a real learning experience for me. We had a ten-acre organic garden and three full-time gardeners (and a Kubota tractor). While I had access to many fresh vegetables and herbs—which was wonderful—I learned that ten acres is not nearly enough to supply a busy restaurant. While Mudd's was not a Creole restaurant, I had menu flexibility and many opportunities to experiment with Creole specials.

Two poultry dishes from the two most talented and influential female chefs in New Orleans, Susan Spicer and Anne Kearney, launch this chapter.

# boudin-stuffed quail with fig sauce

Chef Susan Spicer of Bayona operates under no proscriptions like those I had at Mudd's and offers up to us this stuffed quail dish. (The last time I ate at Bayona, I had a perfectly cooked chicken dish she stuffed with boudin noir.) Serves 4.

| INGREDIENT | QUANTITY |
|---|---|
| Butter or olive oil | 1 tbsp. |
| Onion, small, finely chopped | ½ |
| Celery, finely chopped | 2 stalks |
| Green onions, finely chopped | 2 |
| Cooked rice | 1 c. |
| Pork boudin (a spicy pork and rice sausage) | 1 lb. |
| Mixed herbs, including sage, thyme and parsley) | 1 tbsp. |
| Salt and pepper | To taste |
| Boneless or semiboneless quail | 8 |
| Softened butter | 1 tbsp. |

### FOR THE SAUCE

| | |
|---|---|
| Shallots, finely chopped | 2 |
| White wine | 1 c. |
| Chicken stock | 1 qt. |
| Thyme leaves, fresh | 1 tsp. |
| Apple cider vinegar | 1 tbsp. |
| Fig preserves | 2 tbsp. |
| Fresh figs, diced | ½ c. |
| Butter, unsalted | 2–3 tbsp. |
| Salt and pepper | To taste |
| Lemon juice | If needed |

## METHOD

1. Preheat oven to 400°.
2. Melt butter or olive oil in a small pan and sweat the onion, celery, and scallion for 2 to 3 minutes.
3. Let cool, then mix with rice in a bowl.
4. Remove boudin from its casing and crumble into rice mixture.
5. Add herbs and seasoning and mix thoroughly.
6. Divide stuffing into 8 equal portions and stuff into quail.
7. Rub each quail with a little butter and season with salt and pepper.
8. When sauce is ready, roast quail for 12 to 15 minutes until golden brown and firm but not dry.
9. Place shallots, wine, and vinegar in a small sauce pot and bring to a boil.
10. Reduce heat and simmer until wine is reduced by at least half.
11. Add stock, bring back to a boil, and reduce to about 1 cup of liquid.
12. Stir in thyme, preserves, and figs and simmer for another 5 minutes or so.
13. Whisk in butter and season to taste with salt and pepper and a squeeze of lemon if sauce is too sweet.
14. Place 2 quail on each plate and nap (nap means to "coat"—but just barely) with sauce.
15. Garnish with fresh roasted figs and lemon thyme.

# squab louisiana

This is pan-seared squab with "dirty rice" dressing and brandy demi-glace reduction. Anne Kearney incorporates her take on a classic southern Louisiana dish—"dirty rice"—in the following recipe. She and I share a fondness for the basmati rice she uses in this preparation. In introducing this dish, I do not think I could improve on what Chef Kearney said to me about it:

"This next dish started off many years ago as a tribute to the Creoles and Acadians of Louisiana. I loved the way 'dirty' rice utilized organs of animals rather than throwing them away. Before our time of excess, people would use all that there was to offer. (I am definitely the queen of utilization.) The French gave the rice dressing the name of dirty because of its look (color). Out of respect for the Acadians and the French I refer to the dish as 'dirty' rice dressing on the menu. I harvest the livers, hearts, and gizzards from each squab, make a base for my rice, then ultimately serve the finished product in a very elegant fashion."

| INGREDIENT | QUANTITY |
|---|---|
| **DIRTY RICE BASE** | |
| Hearts and gizzards cut into ½-inch pieces | 6 oz. |
| Garlic, smashed | 1 clove |
| Bay leaf, large | 1 |
| Kosher salt | ½ tsp. |
| Cayenne | Pinch |
| White pepper | Generous ⅛ tsp. |
| **THE LIVERS** | |
| Livers, trimmed free of sinew and veins, towel dried | 10 oz. |

## METHOD

### DIRTY RICE BASE

1. Place all the ingredients in a small pot, cover with water, bring to a boil, and simmer for 45 minutes.

2. Strain, reserving ⅓ cup of the liquid. Cool slightly.

### SQUAB

1. Remove each side of the bird from the squab, leaving only the leg bones and first digit of the wing.

2. Roast the squab carcasses and wing tips at 450° until caramelized.

3. Wrap each bird (two halves) in a c-fold (paper towel) towel; refrigerate until you are ready to sear for service.

*continued*

## SEASONING MIXTURE

| | |
|---|---|
| Kosher salt | 1½ tsp. |
| White pepper, freshly ground | ¼ tsp. |
| Cayenne | Generous pinch |
| Vegetable oil | 2 tbsp. |
| Onions, diced | ¼ c. |
| Celery, diced | 3 tbsp. |
| Brandy to deglaze | ½ c. |

## BASMATI PILAF

| | |
|---|---|
| Butter, unsalted | 2 tbsp. |
| Yellow onion, small dice | ½ c. |
| Kosher salt | ½–1 tsp. |
| Pepper, white, freshly ground | ¼ tsp. |
| Cayenne, ground | Pinch |
| Basmati rice | 1½ c. |
| Hot poultry stock | 3 c. |

## THE LIVERS

1. Sear the livers in a large hot, hot pan until caramelized and medium in the center. This may have to be done in batches.

2. After the last batch of livers is done, add the onions and celery. Using a wooden spoon, scrape all the fond (literally, "bottom," but this word means a lot more in the professional kitchen. What appears to be "debris" to a home cook is *flavor* to a professional. We deglaze this *fond* and incorporate it in the dish) off the bottom of the pan and cook the vegetables until they are tender and golden.

3. Add the brandy to deglaze and reduce. Add to the livers and cool for 30 minutes.

4. Add the hearts and gizzards to the work bowl of a food processor, then process until a paste. Add the livers and vegetables, then purée until smooth. It will have some texture to it. The texture lends to the dirty rice, really.

(Anne says this may be frozen at this point.)

## BASMATI PILAF

1. Melt butter in a sauce pot, add the onions, and stir to coat. Cook over medium heat until the onions are tender and translucent.

2. Add the rice and stir to coat thoroughly.

3. Add the hot stock, reduce the heat to low, and cover. Cook for 15 minutes and check for doneness. Cook until just al dente.

4. Spread onto a lined ½-sheet tray and cool completely. Store until needed.

To finish the rice dressing you will need to add this mixture under "Finishing the Dish and Presentation" below.

# squab sauce

8 orders

| INGREDIENT | QUANTITY | METHOD |
|------------|----------|--------|
| Vegetable oil | 2 tsp. | 1. Heat the oil in a 2-quart sauce pot. Add the onion, celery, carrots, and garlic and cook until tender and golden. |
| Onions, chopped | ½ c. | |
| Celery, chopped | ¼ c. | |
| Carrot | ¼ c. | 2. Add the brandy (away from the flame; it will ignite) and reduce by half; add the poultry stock, demi-glace, bay leaf, garlic, and peppercorns. |
| Brandy | 2 c. | |
| Poultry stock | 3 c. | |
| Demi-glace | 3 c | 3. Reduce until 2 cups remain. Strain through chinoise and hold in a small pot until you are ready to serve. |
| Bay leaf | 1 | |
| Garlic, smashed | 2 cloves | |
| Black peppercorns | 10 | 4. When you are ready to serve, bring the sauce to a boil, mount with 1 tablespoon cold butter, taste, and adjust the seasonings with kosher salt and freshly ground white pepper. |
| Green onion, minced | About ¾ c. | |
| Parsley, chopped | 1 tbsp. | |
| Poultry stock | 8 oz. | |
| Butter, unsalted | 3 tbsp. | |

## FINISHING THE DISH AND PRESENTATION

1. Season the squab on both sides with salt and pepper.
2. Heat 2 tablespoons vegetable oil in a 12-inch sauté pan, pan-sear the squab, skin side down until the skin is evenly brown and crisp, flip, and sear the flesh side until golden and sealed.
3. Remove from the pan and place on a sheet tray. Fire the squab in a 350° oven and cook for 8minutes. The squab should be medium when it is served. Avoid cooking the squab past medium, as it suffers greatly from drying out.
4. Meanwhile, as the squab cooks, degrease the pan and add 1 ounce stock and 2 tablespoons liver base; mash the liver base into the stock.
5. Add ¾ cup basmati pilaf, 1 tablespoon shaved green onions, 1 teaspoon chopped parsley, 1½ teaspoons unsalted butter, and salt and freshly ground white pepper to taste.
6. Make a mound of dirty rice dressing in the center of your plate, then stand the squab on top. (It looks like the squab is doing a handstand on the rice.) Sauce and serve. Yum.

# *poulet sauté with wild mushrooms*

A few years ago, I had a dish very like this one at a restaurant called Gautreau's (1728 Soniat in the Garden District). I rarely eat chicken in a restaurant, but I liked the looks of the dish. This is strictly my version of it. John Harris, chef/owner of Lilette, not only worked with Susan Spicer at Bayona but was chef at Gautreau's a few years ago when I had this delicious meal.

If you have a very large skillet, you may be able to sauté this dish in one pan. Most folks don't. You will probably require three 10-inch sauté or fry pans or two 14-inch fry pans. As with nearly all sautés, your pan must be of solid metal (no wooden handles) so you may place the pan in the oven. You will, no doubt, note that this recipe involves two other recipes in the book—the velouté and the purée of garlic potatoes.

| INGREDIENT | QUANTITY | METHOD |
|---|---|---|
| Chickens, 2½ lb., approximately, quartered | 2 | 1. Disjoint the chickens. Trim off the last two wing joints. |
| Flour | 1 c. | 2. Thoroughly dry the chickens and dredge the pieces in the flour to which you have added the salt and pepper to taste. |
| Salt | To taste | |
| Pepper, white | To taste | |
| Clarified butter or extra virgin olive oil | 6–8 oz. | 3. Heat the butter or oil until quite hot. Caramelize the chicken on both sides and then place your pans in a 500° oven for about 15 minutes. |
| Dry white wine | 12–16 oz. | 4. When the chicken is about 5 minutes from being finished, add the white wine and the lemon juice to the pan(s) and replace the pans in the oven. |
| Lemon juice | 3–4 tbsp. | |
| Chicken velouté (see page 18) | 1½ c. | 5. Remove the pans from the oven and remove the chicken from the pans. |
| Heavy cream | 1–1½ c. | |
| Wild mushrooms (shiitake, shimeji, etc.) | 4–6 oz. | 6. Stew the mushrooms in the butter, wine, and lemon juice mixture. Reduce the liquid by half on top of the stove. Add the heavy cream. Add the velouté (see page 18). |
| | | 7. Check the seasoning and serve with the Purée of Garlic Potatoes (see page 166). |

**LAGNIAPPE** - You may buy a dried wild mushroom mix and reconstitute them in hot water.

# poulet roti with spiced crab apples
## (roasted chicken with spiced crab apples)

All of our modern cultivated cooking, eating, and cider apples were derived from the crab apple species. (You realize this means Adam and Eve ate a crab apple.) The fruits are smaller than cultivated apples and tend to be sour. Since the best cooking apples have this latter characteristic also, they are a good ingredient for many dishes where you would use a cultivated apple. They are often made into jams and jellies or candied. If there are no fresh crab apples available in your area I have seen them on the Internet available in 10-pound lots. Also, many supermarkets have them available in 16-ounce jars. "Spicing" them, though, is a fairly quick procedure. See recipe on page 112. Serves 8.

| INGREDIENT | QUANTITY |
|---|---|
| Chickens, fryers, whole | 2 |
| Salt | To taste |
| Pepper, black, freshly ground | To taste |
| Butter, unsalted, softened | ½ lb. |
| Onion, diced | 1½ c. |
| Andouille sausage, skinned | 1 lb. |
| Spiced crab apples without syrup | 1 lb. |
| Steen's Cane Syrup | ½ c. |
| Port | ½ c. |
| Crab apple syrup | 1 c. |

### METHOD

1. Salt and pepper the chickens.
2. Loosen the skin over the breasts and work some of the softened butter up under the skin. Rub the chickens all over with butter.
3. Heat the remaining butter in a sauté pan and add the onions. Cook until translucent.
4. Crumble the sausage into the pan.
5. Cut the crab apples into chunks and add them to the pan. Add cane syrup. Drain.
6. Stuff chickens loosely with this mixture and commence fowl bondage, trussing the legs tightly over the sewn-shut cavity.
7. Tuck the wingtips up under the chickens.
8. Place the chickens in a tight-fitting roasting pan you have buttered.
9. Pour the port and syrup in the pan. (Add a little chicken stock if the liquid does not come up at least one inch on the chickens.)
10. Roast in a 450° oven for about 1½ hours basting with the pan juices occasionally.
11. Garnish with whole spiced crab apples.

# spiced crab apples

| INGREDIENT | QUANTITY |
|---|---|
| Crab apples | 5 lb. |
| Water | 12 oz. |
| Lemon zest | 1 tbsp. |
| Granulated sugar | 1 lb. |
| Red wine vinegar | 16 oz. |
| Cinnamon stick | 2–3 |
| Cloves, whole | 4–5 |
| Whole black peppercorns | 6 |
| Fresh ginger, peeled, minced | 1 tbsp. |

## METHOD

1. Wash the crab apples. Place water in a pot and add the lemon zest, sugar, and red wine vinegar. Bring the mixture to a boil.

2. Place crab apples in the pot and reduce to a simmer.

3. Place all remaining spices in cheesecloth, tie securely and place in the pot.

4. Simmer for about 30 minutes (check the apples periodically—time will depend on size).

5. Remove cheesecloth and use immediately or chill in syrup. They will remain wholesome for several days in the refrigerator.

**LAGNIAPPE** - These make a great garnish for braised meat dishes. In restaurants I have frequently garnished sauerbraten and rouladen with them.

# sweetbreads madeira

Sweetbreads are among my favorite dishes when prepared well. This is a simple but elegant dish much like one made at Corinne Dunbar's. Serves 6.

> **LAGNIAPPE -** Sweetbreads are the thymus glands of young animals. We are speaking of veal here. They are located in the throat and near the heart. Choose sweetbreads that are white, plump, and firm. They're very perishable and should be prepared within 24 hours of purchase. Soak them in acidulated water (with lemon juice) for about an hour in the refrigerator. Remove the outer membrane.

| INGREDIENT | QUANTITY |
|---|---|
| Veal sweetbreads, cleaned | 1½ lb. |
| Flour | 1 c. |
| Salt | 1 tsp. |
| Freshly ground black pepper | ½ tsp. |
| Eggs, lightly beaten | 2 |
| Butter, unsalted | 4 oz. |
| Madeira wine | ½ c. |

## BROWN SAUCE

| INGREDIENT | QUANTITY |
|---|---|
| Clarified butter, unsalted | 6 oz. |
| Flour | 6 tbsp. |
| Beef stock | 2 c. |
| Salt | To taste |
| Freshly ground black pepper | To taste |

## METHOD

1. Blanch the sweetbreads in simmering water for approximately 10 minutes. Drain, and allow to cool.

2. Make the brown roux by heating the butter and stirring in the flour. Cook over low heat, stirring constantly, until the roux turns a medium brown, about 15 to 20 minutes. Add the stock, salt and pepper to taste.

3. Slice the cooked sweetbreads in half. Dredge them in the flour seasoned with 1 tsp. of salt and ½ tsp. of black pepper, and then in the eggs.

4. Immediately sauté the sweetbreads in the butter and brown both sides. Drain half the butter from the pan, and place the sweetbreads and remaining butter into a hot, 475° oven for 5 minutes. Drain the remaining butter.

5. Add half of the Madeira (¼ c.) and 1 c. of the brown sauce to the sweetbreads and bring to a simmer. Pour in the remainder of the Madeira and flambé. Add the rest of the brown sauce, heat and serve.

*creole nouvelle*

# chicken pontalba brennan's

This is a well-known dish from Brennan's. I think it dates from the 1950's. Supposedly named after a "Baroness" who was something of a New Orleans character. Among other things her father-in-law shot her a number of times. Serves 8.

| INGREDIENT | QUANTITY |
|---|---|
| Chicken breasts, boned, skinned, and halved | 8 |
| Butter | 2 tsp. |
| Butter | ½ c. |
| Salt | ¾ tsp. |
| Pepper | Dash |
| Water | for poaching |
| Garlic, finely chopped | 4 tbsp. |
| White onions, chopped | 2 c. |
| Green onions, chopped | 2 c. |
| Boiled ham, chopped | 1½ c. |
| Mushroom, sliced | 2 c. |
| Diced potatoes | 1½ c. |
| Parsley, chopped | 3 tbsp. |
| White wine | ¾ c. |
| Béarnaise sauce | 3 c. |

## METHOD

1. Deep fry diced potatoes for about 2 minutes.

2. In a large sauté pan or skillet put in the 2 tbsp. butter, salt, pepper, and add about ¼ inch water to the pan. Bring this poaching liquid to the boil, add chicken breasts, cover, lower heat and simmer 15 minutes or until the breasts are done. With a slotted spoon remove the breasts and keep warm in 200° oven. Discard the poaching liquid.

3. In another sauté pan or skillet, melt the remaining butter and sauté the garlic, onions, ham, and mushrooms until they are brown. Add the wine and reduce by one-third. Add fried potatoes and parsley and cook 2 minutes. Remove and keep warm in the oven.

4. To assemble the Pontalba, put ⅛ of the potato/ham mixture in the center of the plate. Place on each side of the mixture ½ of a chicken breast. Top each breast with a generous amount of Béarnaise sauce.

# chicken rochambeau

Similar to Eggs Hussarde in that it incorporates both Marchand de Vin and Béarnaise, a sauce derivative of Hollandaise, this dish is an Antoine's classic. This is an excellent way to utilize leftover roast chicken or turkey. Serves 6.

| INGREDIENT | QUANTITY |
|---|---|
| French or Italian bread, toasted | 6 slices |
| Roast chicken or turkey | 6 healthy slices |
| Lightly smoked ham | 4 large slices |
| Parsley, minced | 1 tbsp. |
| Worcestershire | Dash |
| Salt and pepper | To taste |
| Béarnaise sauce | 1 c. |
| Marchand de Vin sauce | 1 c. |

**METHOD**

1. Sauté the ham and warm the chicken slices.

2. Place the toast on the plate, then the ham, then a generous amount of Marchand de Vin sauce, then the chicken, then top with the Béarnaise sauce. Garnish with parsley.

# cassoulet

Anatole France is among the writers who have extolled the virtues of this most expensive of bean dishes. It is believed the dish originated in the province of Languedoc. Yet there is considerable discussion that it may have gotten its start in Toulouse, Castelnaudary, or Carcassone. If you drew a line due southeast from Toulouse to the Mediterranean, it would go through all three cities.

All three versions of the dish contain beans, pork, ham, and bacon. The cassoulet of Castelnaudary might have mutton and/or partridge included as well. Baked beans à la Toulouse is probably the most distinguished of the three, for it contains confit d'oie (preserved goose) and sausages. Why the confit d'oie?

In Toulouse, they rear a large grosse (goose), primarily to obtain its fatted liver for foie gras. The flesh of this big bird is quite unsuitable for roasting, and rather than leave the countryside littered with the carcasses of rotting fowl, the inhabitants turn the goose cadavers into confit d'oie. I use the more readily obtainable duck for my cassoulet.

I classify this dish as "braised" instead of "baked" because I brown the meats and fowl before I add a liquid.

The dish was brought to Louisiana by the original Creoles, many of whom had antecedents in the southwest of France. You may use John Harris's confit (page 70) in this dish instead of the fresh duckling.

---

**LAGNIAPPE** - Beans, boiled and soaked: Bring the beans to a boil in ample water, boil for 5 minutes, place a lid on the pot, and allow the beans to rest for 1 hour.

---

| INGREDIENT | QUANTITY | INGREDIENT | QUANTITY |
|---|---|---|---|
| Pork shoulder, roasted, visible fat removed | 2–3 lb. | Garlic, minced | ¼ c. |
| Small white beans, boiled and soaked | 2 lb. | Tomatoes, peeled, seeded, diced | 3 c. |
| Duck, disjointed and sautéed | 1 | Bay leaf | 4 |
| Bacon, cut into Lardons and sautéed | 1 lb. | Thyme, whole | 1 tbsp. |
| Sausage, spicy, whatever you like | 1½ lb. | Dry white wine | 3 c. |
| Ham, lightly smoked, medium dice | ½ lb. | Brown stock | 1 qt. |
| Onion, sliced thinly, sautéed in butter | 2 c. | Brandy | ¼ c. |
| | | Salt | 1 tbsp. |
| | | Pepper | To taste |

## METHOD

1. Cut the pork shoulder into 2-inch squares.

2. Discard the water in which the beans were boiled and soaked.

3. Place the beans in a stockpot with the duck back, half the bacon, two or three pieces of the pork, three or four slices of the sausage, half the ham, the onions, the garlic, tomatoes, bay leaf, thyme, wine, brown stock, brandy, salt, and pepper. Bring to a boil and simmer for 1½ hours.

4. Beginning with the beans, make alternating layers of the beans and various meats in a casserole. Pour in just enough of the liquid to come to the top.

5. Cover the top with the mixture of bread crumbs and parsley and dot with butter.

6. Bake in a 425° oven for about 30 minutes, crack the crust that has formed, and push it gently into the casserole. Cover the top again with the bread crumb and parsley mixture and dot with butter.

7. Bake for an additional 20 to 30 minutes or until the crust forms again. Serve in the casserole.

# chicken creole

The first few steps of this dish are identical to the Poulet Sauté on page 110. This dish has probably been around as long as there have been chickens and Creoles. It is, though, a very light dish but not light on flavor.

| INGREDIENT | QUANTITY | METHOD |
|---|---|---|
| Chickens, 2½ lb., approximately, quartered | 2 | 1. Disjoint the chickens. Trim off the last two wing joints. |
| Flour | 1 c. | 2. Thoroughly dry the chickens and dredge the pieces in the flour to which you have added the salt and pepper to taste. Shake off excess. |
| Salt | To taste | |
| Pepper, white | To taste | 3. Heat the butter or oil until quite hot. Caramelize the chicken on both sides and then place your pans in a 500° oven for about 15 minutes. |
| Clarified butter or extra virgin olive oil | 6–8 oz. | |
| Dry white wine | 12–16 oz. | 4. When the chicken is about 5 minutes from being finished, add the white wine to the pan(s) and replace the pans in the oven. |
| Creole sauce (see page 23) | 3–4 c. | |
| | | 5. Remove pans from oven and place on medium heat on stovetop and ladle in Creole sauce. Check seasoning and serve with rice or noodles. |

# chicken clemenceau

This is a dish you will find on the menus of nearly all the older Creole restaurants. Just about the only thing the various versions have in common is the fact that they all contain chicken, some kind of fried potato, and peas. Not only that, but everyone who agrees there are "Brabant Potatoes" in the dish disagrees about just what they are. (*The Fannie Farmer Cookbook* published in 1918 has them as a baked dish.) I do know Brabant was once a European duchy that is now in five pieces divided up among Belgium and the Netherlands. Whatever, I like the Brabant Potatoes in the dish. We will not blanch them in water as most recipes ask you to do (some recipes say "Boil some potatoes and then fry them"), but, rather, we will fry them twice as we do with classic fried potatoes. In fact, let's start with the Brabant Potatoes. Serves 6 to 8.

> **LAGNIAPPE** - Georges Clemenceau was an interesting guy. Twice French prime minister, he held office during the World War I. He lived in the United States for a while right after our Civil War. I have no idea who named this dish after him or why.

| INGREDIENT | QUANTITY |
|---|---|
| **BRABANT POTATOES** | |
| Russet (Idaho) potatoes, peeled | 4 lb. |
| Water, cold | To cover |
| Sugar, granulated | 2 tsp. |
| Peanut oil | 2 qt. |
| Kosher salt | To taste |

## METHOD

1. Block the potatoes off into a rectangular shape. Dice into ¾" square pieces and place in a bowl of cold water in which you have dissolved the sugar.

2. Heat the peanut oil to 350°. Remove the potatoes from the water and thoroughly dry them.

3. Fry the potatoes in the oil for about 4 to 5 minutes. Remove and drain. They will not be brown or crisp yet. Don't worry. You are going to finish these near the end of the Chicken Clemenceau. (You may prepare the potatoes up to this point hours ahead if you choose.)

*continued*

## CHICKEN CLEMENCEAU

| | |
|---|---|
| Chicken, fryers, cut in quarters | 2 |
| Olive oil, extra virgin | ½ c. |
| Salt | To taste |
| Pepper, black, freshly ground | To taste |
| Butter, unsalted | ¼ c. |
| Oyster mushrooms, separated | ¼ lb. |
| Ham, lightly smoked, julienned | ¼ lb. |
| Garlic, minced | 1 tsp. |
| Fresh peas, small | ½ lb. |
| Brabant potatoes | 1 recipe |
| Béarnaise sauce (see recipe page 20) | 1 recipe |

## METHOD

1. Preheat the oven to 450°. Dry the chicken and heat the olive oil in a frypan.

2. Salt and pepper the chicken and sauté it until it is golden brown.

3. Turn the chicken with its skin side down in the fry pan and place in the oven for 15 minutes.

4. Melt the butter in another fry pan.

5. Add the mushrooms and sweat for a couple of minutes.

6. Add ham and garlic and sweat for an additional minute.

7. Add peas to pan and cook for 2 to 3 minutes.

8. Heat the peanut oil to 360°.

9. Fry potatoes again until they are golden and crisp. Drain and salt immediately.

10. Add the peas and potatoes. Sauté for 3 to 4 minutes.

11. The 15 minutes should have elapsed by now. Remove the chicken from the oven. The skin side (bottom) should be a handsome golden brown. This will be your presentation side.

12. Cover each plate with the Brabant potatoes. Make a well in the center of the plate and spoon the mushroom, ham, garlic and pea mixture into the well.

13. Place the chicken on the mushroom mixture.

14. Nap the chicken with the Béarnaise.

# grillades

This New Orleans Swiss or braised steak dish happens to be among my favorites. It is usually served with rice or grits. The name of the dish, however, is something of a misnomer. The French word *grillade* means "grilling" or "broiling" or a grilled steak. Yet I have never seen a recipe for grillades (gree-odds) in which the meat was grilled. The dish is, as with all braised dishes, cooked quickly in fat, then slowly with a liquid. In New Orleans the dish is sometimes made with veal, which seems a waste to me since the strong flavors of the spicing would totally obliterate any subtlety the veal might possess.

This technique, braising, utilizes the less expensive cuts of meat and involves a long cooking time. This is a technique I strongly stress to my students since most of any animal is not tender. Additionally, the tougher cuts of meat can have more character and flavor.

There were examples of braised dishes featured on every menu of the five restaurants presented in chapter 11. They were quite creatively employed—and not just as a main course.

| INGREDIENT | QUANTITY |
|---|---|
| Clarified butter or cooking oil | ½ c. |
| Beef, eye of round | 3–4 lb. |
| Pepper, black, finely ground | 1 tsp. |
| Pepper, white, finely ground | 1 tsp. |
| Cayenne, finely ground | 1 tsp. |
| Salt | 1 tbsp. |
| Flour | 1 c. |
| Onion, yellow, diced medium | 1½ c. |
| Bell pepper, diced medium | 1½ c. |
| Celery, diced medium | 1½ c. |
| Garlic, minced | 1 tbsp. |
| Tomatoes, peeled and seeded | 3 c. |
| Tomato purée | 1 c. |
| Bay leaves | 3 or 4 |
| Thyme, whole | 1 tbsp. |
| Brown stock (see page 12) | 1 qt. |
| Brown roux (see page 14) | Approx. ½ c. |

**METHOD**

1. Slowly heat butter or oil in a large skillet.
2. While the oil is heating, slice the eye of round, across the grain, into ½-inch-thick slices.
3. Place the slices between layers of plastic wrap and pound them until they are between ⅛ and ¼ inch thick. Try not to tear them.
4. Combine black, white, and red peppers with salt and flour in a shallow bowl.
5. Thoroughly dry the beef and dredge both sides in the flour mixture.
6. Sauté the beef in the butter or oil until well browned on both sides. Remove.
7. Sauté onion, bell pepper, and celery until lightly browned. Add garlic.
8. Add tomatoes, tomato purée, bay leaf, and thyme.
9. Add stock.
10. Place mixture in a roasting pan or casserole with a cover, place beef in this mixture, and cover.
11. Cook in a 375° oven for approximately 45 minutes or until beef is tender enough to be cut with a fork.
12. Remove beef from sauce when done and incorporate just enough roux to thicken slightly. Return meat to sauce.
13. Serve with grits or rice.

# savory latino roasted pork with very comfortable black beans and green olive manchego hallaca

Here's a Latin influenced dish created by Chef Peter Vazquez of Marisol. This is a dish with many steps. It will require a little forethought and a few ingredients you may not have in your kitchen. You should be able to obtain all the ingredients at a local Latin market.

| INGREDIENT | QUANTITY |
|---|---|
| **THE MARINATION** | |
| Boneless Boston pork butt | 2 lb. |
| Garlic | 4 cloves |
| Onion, medium | 1 |
| Southern Comfort | ¼ c. |
| Lime juice | ¼ c. |
| Orange juice | ¼ c. |
| Olive oil | 3 tbsp. |
| Salt | 1 tbsp. |
| Saffron, dissolved in warm water | 1 pinch |
| **PREPARATION** | |
| Lard or olive oil | 3 tbsp. |
| Onion, large, yellow, finely diced | 1 |
| Garlic, minced | 5 cloves |
| Red bell pepper, seeded and finely diced | 1 |
| Green bell pepper, seeded and finely diced | 1 |
| Tomato, large, chopped | 1 |
| Oregano | 1 tsp. |
| Salt | 1 tbsp. |
| Chicken or pork stock | 3 c. |
| Southern Comfort | ¼ c. |

| INGREDIENT | QUANTITY |
|---|---|
| **BEANS** | |
| Dry black beans, soaked overnight | 2 c. |
| Cumin | 1 tbsp. |
| Onion, medium, diced | 1 |
| Tomato, large, chopped | 1 |
| Garlic, minced | 3 cloves |
| Southern Comfort | ½ c. |
| Chicken or pork stock | 7 c. |
| Lime juice | ¼ c. |
| Orange juice | ¼ c. |
| Salt | 1 tbsp. |
| Pepper, black | 3 tbsp. |
| **HALLACAS** | |
| White hominy | 1 can |
| Annatto seed (optional) | 2 tsp. |
| Lard | 1 oz. |
| Salt | ½ tbsp. |
| Pitted green olives, chopped | 1 c. |
| Onion, minced | 4 tbsp. |
| Garlic, minced | 1 tsp. |
| Chicken stock | 1 tbsp. |
| Tomato purée | 1 tbsp. |
| Golden raisins, softened in hot water | 4 tbsp. |
| Manchego cheese, cubed | 4 oz. |
| Banana leaf, large | 1 |

# METHOD

## THE MARINATION

1. Place pork in a nonreactive container (glass or stainless steel).

2. Combine all other ingredients in a food processor or blender and process until smooth.

3. Cover pork with mixture and marinate overnight.

## PREPARATION

1. Preheat oven to 300°.

2. Heat fat in a heavy casserole until very hot.

3. Remove pork from marinade and sear on all sides until golden brown.

4. Reserve marinade.

5. Remove pork from pan and add remaining ingredients (except stock and Southern Comfort), then lower heat and cook for about 30 minutes until thick.

6. Return pork to mixture in casserole.

7. Add marinade, stock, and remaining Southern Comfort, then cover and place in oven for 4 to 5 hours until tender.

8. Reserve and keep warm.

## HALLACAS

1. Melt lard and cook annatto seeds until well colored. Remove seeds.

2. Heat 1 tablespoon of the lard in a sauté pan and add salt, olives, onion, and garlic.

3. Grind hominy with remaining lard and ½ tablespoon of salt.

4. Cut banana into four squares, 8 by 8 inches.

5. Divide hominy dough among the four banana squares.

6. Top hominy with 2 tablespoons of the olive mixture and 1 ounce of the cheese.

7. Fold leaf over filling, fold leaf ends over, place in steamer, and steam for 30 minutes. Keep warm.

# PRESENTATION

1. Place one hallaca in center of plate and unfold leaf.

2. Slice or shred pork over hallaca and spoon some of the juices over.

3. Spoon beans around hallaca and serve.

4. Drink remaining Southern Comfort.

**LAGNIAPPE** - Hallacas (ay-YAH-kahs) come to us from Colombia and Venezuela; they are South America's variation on tamales. They usually consist of ground beef, pork, or chicken mixed with other foods, such as cheese, olives, or raisins, surrounded by a ground-corn dough, wrapped in banana leaves, and steamed or boiled.

# braised lamb shanks creole

Lamb shanks are right at the top of my list for my favorite braised dishes. I had an excellent interpretation from Peter Vazquez at Marisol the last time I ate there. The following is my Creole adaptation of a traditional French bistro dish. Serves 6.

| INGREDIENT | QUANTITY |
|---|---|
| Garlic cloves, large, peeled | 6 |
| Lamb shanks | 6 |
| Kosher salt | To taste |
| Pepper, black, freshly ground | To taste |
| All-purpose flour | 1 c. |
| Olive oil, extra virgin | ½ c. |
| Carrots, large, diced | 3 |
| Onions, medium, peeled and quartered | 2 |
| Bell peppers, red and green, diced | 1 of each |
| Dry red wine | 2 c. |
| Fresh thyme sprig | 1 |
| Fresh basil, minced | 1 tbsp. |
| 28 oz. can Roma tomatoes with juice | 1 |
| Beef or chicken stock | 1½ cups |

## METHOD

1. Slice the garlic cloves vertically. With a paring knife make small incisions in the meaty part of the shanks. Insert the garlic cloves in the incisions.

2. Dry the shanks and salt and pepper them. Dredge them in the flour and shake off the excess.

3. In a thick-bottomed pot get the olive oil quite hot and brown the lamb shanks completely. Remove them from the pot and set aside.

4. Sauté the carrots, onions, peppers, and celery in the oil until light brown.

5. Deglaze with the red wine, scraping the bottom of the pot to incorporate all fonds.

6. Add thyme, basil, tomatoes, and stock.

7. Cover and place in a 350° oven for 2 to 2½ hours, stirring occasionally.

   Serve with the Risotto Milanese (see page 164) or the Purée of Garlic Potatoes (see page 166) or on a bed of the Stewed White Haricot on page 125.

# stewed white haricot

This bean has a bunch of names—Great Northern bean, canellini, and white kidney bean are a few. Often served with braised dishes, it makes a great accompaniment to the Braised Lamb Shanks on page 124. Beans have to their credit, in addition to the mellifluous organic homage they accord Calliope, the fact that they are among the most nutritional foods out there. I like them a lot. Serves 8.

**LAGNIAPPE** - You will run across "Calliope" street in New Orleans. It is not "ka-lye-uh-pee." Pronounce it "kal-ee-ope." Emphasis on first and last syllables.

| INGREDIENT | QUANTITY |
|---|---|
| Dried canellini beans | 1 lb. |
| Olive oil, extra virgin | ½ c. |
| Green bell pepper, diced | 1 |
| Red bell pepper, diced | 1 |
| Garlic, minced | 1 tbsp. |
| Stock, beef or chicken | 1 qt. |
| Fresh sage, minced | 1 tsp. |
| Roma tomatoes, canned, diced w/juice | 2 c. |
| Kosher salt | To taste |
| Pepper, black, freshly ground | To taste |
| Tabasco | To taste |

## METHOD

1. Bring the beans to a boil in ample (lots!) water. Boil for 5 minutes, cover tightly, remove from heat and allow to steep for one hour. Check beans for softness. If still firm, bring to a boil again and repeat to steeping procedure for an additional 20 minutes. Drain beans.

2. Heat the olive oil in a pot large enough to hold all ingredients and sweat the peppers until soft. Add garlic and sweat for a minute or so.

3. Add all other ingredients and simmer, covered, for 30 minutes. If you still have a lot of liquid in the beans, simmer uncovered and reduce.

# creole daubes

One could not write a Creole cookbook without including a Creole daube, which is another in a long line of French words for "stew." This dish, though, is more "pot roast" than a stew. Matters not; the technique is the same. The following is really two recipes—the first for a hot and hearty stew and the second for a truly unique traditional Creole dish. This is my version of this favorite winter braised dish. Definitely a one-pot meal—just add a bread. Given the number of steps involved, I strongly suspect that even the most ardent and assiduous Creole cuisine devotees among you will not be making this dish on a weekly basis.

| INGREDIENT | QUANTITY |
|---|---|
| Salt pork | ¼ lb. |
| Beef, rump or chuck | 4–5 lb. |
| Salt | 1 tbsp. |
| Pepper, black, freshly ground | 1 tbsp. |
| Cayenne | 1 tsp. |
| Garlic, very finely minced | 1 tbsp. |
| Fresh thyme | 2 sprigs |
| Olive oil, extra virgin | ½ c. |
| Onion, thinly sliced | 3 c. |
| Carrots, peeled and cut into 1-inch cubes | 1½ c. |
| Turnips, peeled and cut into 1-inch cubes | 1½ c. |
| Dry red wine | 2 c. |
| Stock, white or brown | 1 qt. |
| Kalamata olives, pitted | 1½ c. |
| Bay leaves | 4 |
| Parsley | 2 sprigs |

**METHOD**

1. Cut salt pork into julienne strips ¼ by ¼ inch—about 2 to 3 inches long.

2. I am going to teach you how to "lard" now. This is an ancient method of adding fat and flavor to the tougher cuts of meat. Combine the salt, pepper, cayenne, minced garlic, and half the thyme (remove the leaves from the stems first) and place on a plate. Roll the strips of salt pork in this mixture.

3. Using a knife with a slender blade, such as a paring or boning knife, make deep incisions in the beef. Wiggle your knife around a little to enlarge the hole. Plunge the salt pork strips into these incisions. Get tough. You have just "larded" your meat.

4. Dry the beef thoroughly and rub the outside with salt and pepper.

5. Get the olive oil quite hot in a brazier or large casserole.

6. Brown the beef on all sides in the olive oil. Remove.

7. Add onions first, then carrots and turnips. Caramelize lightly. Remove.

8. Deglaze pot with red wine and return beef to pot. Be sure to scrape up the goodies on the bottom of the pot. Add stock.

9. Add remaining sprig of thyme (whole), kalamata olives, bay leaves, and 1 sprig of parsley.

10. Bring pot to a boil, reduce to a simmer, cover tightly, and cook for approximately 2 hours. The meat should be relatively tender by that time. Add the vegetables back into the pot. Cover and simmer for an additional hour.

11. Remove all solids from pot and reduce pan juices by half. Return all solids to pot and warm through.

12. Place the meat in the center of a platter and surround with the vegetables. Serve with just about any potato dish or noodles or even rice. Either remove the bay leaves (best action) or tell your guests not to eat them, as they will come out looking just like they did when they went in, only considerably more painfully.

# daube glace

To make the glace, you will need to first make the Creole daube on page 126 in its entirety.

Alternatively, you may turn the above into the following Creole classic that goes by several different names: daube froide à la Creole, daube glace, and daube glacee are among them. We do need a name, so we will call it daube Glace.

| INGREDIENT | QUANTITY | METHOD |
|---|---|---|
| Veal round | 3–4 lb. | 1. Add veal to boiling water along with all other ingredients. Return to boil, reduce to a simmer, and cook for 3 to 4 hours until veal and pig's feet are tender. |
| Water, boiling | 5 or 6 qt. | |
| Pigs feet | 2 | |
| Dry red wine | 1 c. | 2. Remove meats from pot and mince finely, removing any skin or tough connective tissue. |
| Bay leaves | 2 | |
| Garlic, minced | 2 cloves | 3. Reduce liquid in pot over high heat until you have about 7 or 8 cups. It should be quite gelatinous at this point. |
| Cayenne | 1 tsp. | |
| Salt | 1 tbsp. | |
| Pepper, black, freshly ground | 1 tsp. | 4. The best presentation for this dish will be in some kind of rectangular pan—a loaf pan or, if you have one, a paté or terrine pan. Many folks just use a bowl, though. |
| Thyme sprig | 1 | |
| Onions, minced | 1 c. | |

5. Whatever container you select, place a layer of the daube in it. (If the beef has not completely fallen apart, shred it now.) Place a layer of the minced veal and pig's feet over this. Pour the gelatinous contents of the pot over these until your container is full. Refrigerate for at least 12 hours.

6. After unmolding onto a platter, the daube glace is then sliced thinly and served with bread and butter or Creole mustard.

**LAGNIAPPE** - If you have trouble finding the pig's feet, 1) you are probably not in the southern United States, and 2) you may substitute powdered gelatin or sheets of gelatin. (The main contribution of the pig's feet is their gelatin.)
You will need to remove some of the liquid (a cup or two) from the veal pot and chill it to room temperature. Add about 1 ounce of gelatin to this cooled liquid and incorporate thoroughly. Pour this back into your 7 or 8 cups of liquid and proceed as above.
Bon chance!

# blanquette de veau

I first had this dish in 1968. A lovely lady prepared it in Bellevue, France. She and her husband were kind enough to put me up—and put up with me—for a couple of days while I was traveling through Europe. Early on the morning of the day she prepared this dish, I went to the market with her to buy the ingredients for this dish. My first experience with a French market was an eye-opening event. Although this was a small town, there were vendors with dozens of kinds of produce, poultry, meats, and dairy products. In the 19th century, veal was a very common meat in the original New Orleans Creole cooking.

## INGREDIENT

| INGREDIENT | QUANTITY |
|---|---|
| Veal, rump, rib eye, or shoulder, 1½-inch cubes | 3 lb. |
| Stock, veal or chicken | 1½ qt. |
| Carrot, quartered | 1 |
| Onion, peeled, medium, stuck with a few cloves | 1 |
| Bouquet garni (see page below) | |
| Boiling onions | 6–8 |
| Mushroom caps, small | 12–16 |
| Butter, unsalted | 6 tbsp. |
| Flour, all-purpose | 6 tbsp. |
| White pepper | To taste |
| Salt | To taste |
| Lemon juice | 3 tbsp. |
| Egg yolks | 4 |
| Heavy cream | 1 c. |

## METHOD

1. Place veal in a saucepan or casserole and cover with the stock. Bring to the boil and skim.
2. Add carrot and onion to the pot. Wrap parsley, thyme, bay leaf, and celery in cheesecloth, then tie and add to pot.
3. Cover and simmer for about 1¼ hours. Do not over cook.
4. Add boiling onions to pot and simmer for 15 minutes.
5. Add mushrooms to pot and simmer for 5 minutes.
6. Melt butter in a sauté pan. Add flour and make a blond roux.
7. Remove veal, onion, carrot, bouquet garni, boiling onions, and mushrooms from stock. Discard carrot, large onion, and bouquet garni.
8. Incorporate roux into stock with a wire whip. Add lemon.
9. In a mixing bowl, beat together the eggs yolks and cream.
10. Beat about 8 ounces of the sauce into the egg mixture to temper the eggs. Add this mixture to the pot and whip thoroughly.
11. Return veal, boiling onions, and mushrooms to the sauce. Check the seasoning and keep warm until ready to serve. Do not boil.

**LAGNIAPPE** - Bouquet garni may be almost any combination of herbs, spices, and vegetables, either tied together or bound in cheesecloth, but for this recipe we will use the following:

| | |
|---|---|
| Parsley | 2 sprigs |
| Thyme | 1 tsp. |
| Bay leaves | 2 |
| Basil leaves | 4 |
| Celery, cut in 2-inch lengths | 2 stalks |

# roasted rack of lamb with minted fig glaze

Rack of lamb has been one of the most popular dishes in restaurants I have done over the years. Try to find the fresh figs for this dish if possible.

| INGREDIENT | QUANTITY | METHOD |
|---|---|---|
| 8-Bone Rack of Lamb | 3–4 | 1. Thoroughly dry lamb and season it with salt and pepper. |
| Minted fig glaze (see recipe page 131) | 12 oz. | 2. Heat olive oil in sauté pan over high heat. Place rack of lamb in pan and caramelize on all sides. |
| Salt | 1 tsp. | 3. Paint the racks on both sides with the Minted Fig Glaze |
| Pepper, black | To taste | Place on the bottom of a pre-heated 450° degree oven for 8–10 minutes for medium rare temperature. |
| Olive oil, extra virgin | 3 tbsp. | |

# minted fig glaze

| INGREDIENT | QUANTITY |
|---|---|
| Water | 1 c. |
| Granulated sugar | 1 c. |
| Fresh mint leaves | 1 c. |
| Fresh figs, minced or fig preserves | 1 c. |
| Steen's cane syrup | ¼ c. |

## METHOD

1. Bring water to a boil and add sugar—simmer to make a simple syrup.

2. As soon as the sugar is completely dissolved add the mint leaves and figs. Simmer for 5 minutes.

3. Remove from heat and push through a sieve. You should have a very thick purée.

4. Add cane syrup and thoroughly incorporate.

5. Using a basting brush, paint the racks with this glaze.

# MORNING IN NEW ORLEANS:
# BREADS AND BREAKFAST DISHES

**B**reads are a key element in Creole cookery, and breakfast is an important meal. The Creoles have always eaten hearty breakfasts. This chapter has the basic method for poaching eggs and making a couple of scrambled egg dishes and the basics of bread baking. Although it is from New York, I have included Eggs Benedict since it is the basis for a few Creole poached egg dishes.

The easiest breakfast/brunch dishes for me are the scrambled egg dishes. We will begin with them.

# bayou brunch

There were several restaurants in the San Francisco Bay Area with the word "Joe's" in their name. "Original Joe's" and "Marin Joe's" are two that come to mind. A version of this dish originated in "Original Joe's." This is my New Orleans adaptation of that dish. It is a good buffet dish for a brunch since it may be made ahead and placed in a chafing dish.

| INGREDIENT | QUANTITY | METHOD |
|---|---|---|
| Butter, unsalted | 2 oz. | 1. Melt butter in a skillet large enough to contain all ingredients. |
| Lean ground beef, 10% fat | 1 lb. | 2. Add ground beef and sauté until browned. Drain fat and return beef to sauté pan. |
| Onions, minced | 1 c. | |
| Garlic, minced | 1 tsp. | 3. Add onions and cook until soft. |
| Mushrooms, thinly sliced | 1 c. | 4. Add garlic and mushrooms. |
| Spinach, washed, dried, julienne | 2 c. | 5. Add spinach and cook until wilted. Allow the water to boil away. |
| Salt | To taste | 6. Add salt and pepper. |
| Pepper, black, freshly ground | To taste | |
| Broken eggs, beaten | 1 dozen | 7. Combine eggs and cream. Add egg mixture, all at one time, and cook over medium heat, stirring constantly, until eggs are just set. |
| Heavy cream | ¼ c. | |
| Sharp cheddar cheese, grated | ½ c. | 8. Place in a chafing dish or on a platter and sprinkle with the cheese. |

# pan-seared oyster scramble

My inspiration for this dish comes from another northern California "scrambled" egg dish. I have substituted Tasso for the original bacon and marinate the oysters in Herbsaint.

That dish is called a "Hangtown Fry." The dish was supposedly invented during the gold rush in California in a town called Vacaville in the Sierra foothills. Here's the story as told to me: A judge in the town had a very tough reputation and was noted for his stiff sentences. Hence, Vacaville came to be called "Hangtown." A condemned man, on being asked what he would like for his final meal, selected items that were quite scarce and expensive, among them oysters, spinach, and eggs. By the time all the ingredients arrived, a pardon from the governor had also arrived, and the sheriff ended up eating the dish.

| INGREDIENT | QUANTITY |
|---|---|
| Butter, unsalted | 4 oz. |
| Oysters | 12–16 |
| Herbsaint | ½ c. |
| Flour, unbleached, all-purpose | 1 c. |
| Salt | To taste |
| Pepper, black, freshly ground | To taste |
| Tasso, thinly sliced | ½ lb. |
| Spinach, washed, dried, and julienned | 2 c. |
| Broken eggs, beaten | 1 dozen |
| Goat cheese, crumbled | 6–8 oz. |

METHOD

1. Melt butter in a skillet large enough to hold all ingredients.

2. Dredge oysters in flour and shake off excess.

3. Add oysters to skillet and sauté until the flour begins to brown. Do not overcook.

4. Add bacon and spinach and sauté until the spinach has wilted.

5. Add eggs and cook until the eggs are just set, stirring constantly.

6. Add cheese to top of dish and melt by placing a lid on the sauté pan and lowering the heat as if for an omelet.

**LAGNIAPPE** - Marinate the oysters in the Herbsaint for at least 30 minutes. You may begin the night before and leave them in the refrigerator overnight.

## POACHING EGGS

The most interesting thing to me about the gadget called an "egg poacher" I see in a lot of home kitchens is that the one thing it does not do is poach eggs. One breaks an egg into an indentation in the gizmo that perches above simmering water. The egg never touches the water, and the white of the egg is invariably tough.

A properly poached egg should have a firm—*not tough*—white and a yolk that is still runny. With a little practice, you should be able to poach six to eight eggs at one time. The water in which we poach must be acidulated, in this instance with *vinegar*, not *lemon juice*. The vinegar will cause the white to draw in. Lemon juice, unfortunately, will cause the white to dissipate.

The poaching is best done in a low-rimmed pan, such as a sautoir, sauté pan, or fry pan. Pour 2 inches of water into the pan and add 1 teaspoon of white vinegar for every 2 cups of water. Bring the water to a boil and reduce to the simmer. Crack the egg on the side of the pan and gently open the shell right at the surface of the liquid. Proceed around the pan until you have 6 to 8 eggs in the water. When the white of the first egg appears firmly set, gently lift it with a slotted spoon or a skimmer. Probe the white with your finger. If it is firm, the egg is cooked. Drain the egg over a cloth towel with which you also lightly daub the top side of the egg. Place the egg on a muffin (see Eggs Hussarde, page 137), toast, plate, or artichoke bottom (see Eggs Sardou, page 138).

# eggs benedict

You are absolutely correct. This is not a New Orleans dish. But you will be hard pressed to find a restaurant serving brunch in this city that does not include it on the menu. That's why I've included it here. Plus, it is the basis for the Eggs Hussarde, a distinctly Creole dish.

| INGREDIENT | QUANTITY | METHOD |
|---|---|---|
| English muffins | 6–8 | 1. Split and toast English muffins. |
| Canadian bacon | 12–16 slices | 2. Grill or sauté Canadian bacon. |
| Poached eggs | 12–16 | 3. Place Canadian bacon on English muffin. |
| Hollandaise sauce | 12–16 oz. | 4. Place one poached egg on each slice of Canadian bacon. |
| | | 5. Ladle the Hollandaise sauce over the poached egg. |

# eggs hussarde

This is a dish conceived at Brennan's. I have eaten and enjoyed it elsewhere. Note you will have to make the Marchand de Vin (page 24) and Hollandaise (page 16) sauces ahead.

| INGREDIENT | QUANTITY |
|---|---|
| English muffins | 6–8 |
| Tomato slices (about ¼ inch thick) | 12–16 |
| Canadian bacon, sliced ¼ inch thick | 12–16 slices |
| Marchand de Vin sauce | 12–16 oz. |
| Poached eggs | 12–16 |
| Hollandaise sauce | 12–16 oz. |

### METHOD

1  Split and toast English muffins.

2. Grill or sauté tomato slices.

3. Grill Canadian bacon.

4. Place Canadian bacon on muffin.

5. Place tomato on bacon.

6. Ladle two ounces of the Marchand de Vin sauce over the tomato.

7. Place poached egg on Marchand de Vin sauce.

8. Ladle hollandaise over poached egg.

# eggs sardou

First served at Antoine's by Antoine himself at a dinner he hosted for Victorien Sardou, a prolific French playwright of the late 19th and early 20th centuries (he died in 1908), this dish now has infinite versions. You will need to make the Hollandaise sauce (page 16) ahead and the artichokes, too, if using fresh. Here's my version of this great brunch dish.

The following quantities may appear somewhat daunting; nothing to worry about, though. Merely cut the recipe in half to serve four.

| INGREDIENT | QUANTITY |
|---|---|
| Butter, unsalted | 4 oz. |
| Baby spinach leaves, washed | 2 lb. |
| Salt and freshly ground black pepper | To taste |
| Heavy cream | 3–4 c. |
| Gruyère cheese, grated | 2 oz. |
| Artichoke bottoms, fresh or canned | 12–16 |
| Simmering water | 3 in. |
| White vinegar | 1 tbsp. |
| Eggs, large | 12–16 |
| Hollandaise sauce | 2–3 c. |
| Parsley, minced | ¼ c. |
| Paprika | Sprinkle |

**METHOD**

1. In a pan large enough to hold all the spinach, melt the butter. Add the spinach, a handful at a time.
2. Cook the spinach until it is wilted. Add salt and pepper. You will have a considerable quantity of water in the pan. Drain off all the water through a colander. Reserve spinach.
3. Place cream in pan and reduce ⅓ over medium heat.
4. Add cheese and melt.
5. Add drained spinach to this mixture and thoroughly incorporate. Set aside and keep warm.
6. Add vinegar to water. Break eggs over water and follow the egg-poaching procedure. Continue until all eggs are poached.
7. While the eggs are poaching, spoon some of the spinach mixture into each of the artichoke bottoms.
8. Drain eggs and place one on top of the spinach mixture on each artichoke.
9. Nap with the hollandaise sauce (I use a 1-ounce ladle).
10. Sprinkle parsley and paprika over all.

**LAGNIAPPE** - This dish is best with fresh artichokes, but I realize one cannot always obtain them. If you use canned artichoke bottoms, all you will need to do is drain and warm them. They are not quite as large as the fresh you will be able to buy, but they will suffice.

Here is the procedure for fresh artichokes: Using a serrated knife, cut off all but about 1½ inches of the bottom of the artichoke. Cut off the stem. Immediately rub all cut surfaces with lemon. Cut remaining leaves off bottom with a paring knife. Remove choke with a spoon or baller. Rub lemon over all again. Bring salted water to a boil. Add artichoke bottoms and poach until a paring knife slips easily into the middle, about 15 minutes. Drain.

# braised duck on buttermilk biscuit with blood orange marmalade

This is a truly nifty dish from Chef Donald Link at Herbsaint. I could not decide where to put it. It is a duck dish but would certainly go well in the New Orleans brunch section here, too. Well, you can make it for whatever meal you want, but I suspect it will end up in your repertoire of morning treats.

This is another of those dishes with several steps, and you might want to plan ahead a little. Make the marmalade a day ahead, and you might consider braising the duck ahead, too. But I would definitely make the biscuits as close to service as possible.

| INGREDIENT | QUANTITY | METHOD |
|---|---|---|
| **DUCK** | | **DUCK** |
| Whole duckling, cut in 8 pieces | 1 | 1. Season duck with spices and lightly sear in olive oil. Move duck into braising pan. |
| Olive oil | ¼ c. | |
| Onion, roughly chopped | 1 c. | 2. Add onions, carrot, celery, and herbs into pan you seared the duck in and sauté until lightly golden. |
| Carrot, roughly chopped | 1 c. | |
| Celery, roughly chopped | 1 c. | 3. Deglaze with white wine, bring to a boil, and add chicken stock. |
| Sage, roughly chopped | ⅓ c. | |
| Thyme, roughly chopped | ⅓ c. | 4. Add all this over the duck in the braising pan and cook covered for about 2 hours at 300°. |
| Rosemary, roughly chopped | ⅓ c. | |
| Red wine | 2 c. | |
| Chicken stock | 1 qt. | |
| Salt, pepper, cayenne, allspice, and fennel combined | 3 tbsp. total | |

*continued*

| INGREDIENT | QUANTITY |
|---|---|
| **BUTTERMILK BISCUITS** | |
| Flour, all-purpose | 3 c. |
| Whole butter | 1 lb. |
| Buttermilk | 1½ c. |
| Baking powder | 1½ tbsp. |
| Salt | 1 tsp. |
| Black pepper | 1 tsp. |

## ORANGE MARMALADE

| Oranges | 2 |
|---|---|
| Lemon, sliced thinly | 1 |
| Sugar | ¾ c. |
| Water | 4 c. |
| Star anise | 1 piece |
| Ground coriander | 1 tsp. |

## METHOD
### BUTTERMILK BISCUITS

1. Mix flour, salt, pepper, and baking powder together.
2. Cut whole butter into flour using a fork and then mix more with your hands.
3. Stir in buttermilk.
4. On a floured work surface, roll the biscuit dough to about 1 inch thick and cut into desired sized circles.
5. Bake at 400° to 425° for about 15 minutes.

### ORANGE MARMALADE

1. Peel the oranges and slice the skin in thin strips, then place in a pot with the seedless inside of the orange and the sliced lemon along with the anise and coriander.
2. Pour the water over the citrus and bring to a boil, then let simmer for 20 minutes.
3. Remove from heat and let cool completely in the fridge. Put back into a pot and simmer another half hour with the sugar and then let the mixture chill overnight. This should allow time for the pectins in the fruit to "jelly."
4. To assemble the dish, pick the meat from the duck and reserve. Cut the biscuit in half and spread the marmalade on the bottom, then place the duck meat on top and top with the other half of the biscuit. If you would like to serve poached eggs, place them on top of the duck and serve with your favorite hollandaise.

Once you have removed the shell the cleaning becomes fairly intuitive.

The beer batter gives the crabs an attractive golden-brown color and distinctive crispness. The Béarnaise (page 20) is the perfect accompaniment.

Try this incredibly rich and lush dish with the fresh artichokes.

A true Creole creation, the stuffed artichoke is a tradition in New Orleans.

Every Monday my mother made red beans and rice—and I looked forward to Monday's.

I know I call this "the world's ugliest cake," but it is with great fondness and many memories.

Top, left to right: Bayona and Marisol; Bottom, left to right: Herbsaint and Lilette.

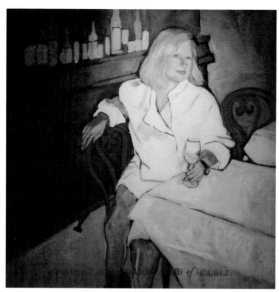

This painting of Anne Kearney graces the end of the bistro-like bar area of Peristyle.

Peristyle

# duck hash

Here is yet another great breakfast/brunch recipe from Chef Donald Link of Herbsaint. It yields 4 to 6 servings.

| INGREDIENT | QUANTITY |
| --- | --- |
| Duck | 1 |
| Salt and pepper | To taste |
| Olive oil | ¼ c. |
| Red wine | ½ c. |
| Onion, chopped | ½ |
| Thyme | 1 sprig |
| Chicken stock | 4 c. |
| Carrot, chopped | 1 |
| Garlic | 3 cloves |

## HASH

| INGREDIENT | QUANTITY |
| --- | --- |
| Butter | 1 tbsp. + 2 tsp. |
| Onion, diced | ¾ c. |
| Bell pepper, diced | ¾ c. |
| Celery, diced | ½ c. |
| Potatoes, diced | ½ c. |
| Garlic, chopped | 1 tsp. |
| Flour | ¼ c. |
| Duck meat | 1½ c. |
| Braising liquid | 1 c. |
| Thyme and sage, fresh | ½ tbsp. each |
| Salt, pepper, and cayenne | To taste |

## METHOD

1. Split the duck in half and season with salt and pepper.
2. Sear the duck in oil to obtain color and render some of the fat.
3. Remove duck from pan and add onion, carrot, garlic, and thyme, then cook until soft and deglaze with red wine and chicken stock.
4. Return the duck to the braising pan cover and cook at 300° for about 2 hours until the duck is soft.
5. When duck is cooled, pick meat from the bone and set aside. Save the braising liquid from the pan.

### HASH

1. Sauté onions, bell peppers, celery, and potatoes in whole butter until soft.
2. Add remaining butter and flour and cook until flour starts to turn brown, add duck meat, and continue cooking and continue to get color on the mix, use braising liquid to deglaze throughout the cooking process.
3. Add seasonings, then let mixture cool. Once cooled, shape the mixture into patties and sear in oil.
   Serve with Poached Eggs and Béarnaise (see page 20).

**LAGNIAPPE** - When sautéing the vegetables, be sure not to overcrowd the pan. Overcrowding makes it very difficult to obtain any color in the dish. An iron skillet is the best pan to cook this in.

# beignets

These are New Orleans "doughnuts." They are *unholy* and, typically, cut into squares or diamonds and dusted with powdered sugar. They were for many years a staple at the Morning Call before it moved to Metairie. If you have time, it will be worth your while. The popular spot in the Quarter now is Café Du Monde.

| INGREDIENT | QUANTITY |
|---|---|
| Whole milk, scalded | 2 c. |
| Shortening | ¼ c. |
| Granulated sugar | ¾ c. |
| Dry yeast | 2 oz. |
| Flour, all-purpose | 5–6 c. |
| Salt | 2 tsp. |
| Eggs, large | 2 |
| Peanut oil | 2 qt. |
| Powdered sugar | As needed |

## METHOD

1. Pour milk over shortening and sugar in a stainless bowl and blend with a wire whip.

2. Cool to about 125° and add yeast. Place in mixer bowl.

3. Run mixer slowly and add about ½ of the flour.

4. Add eggs, one at a time, and salt.

5. Add remaining flour. Allow to rise in an oiled bowl covered with plastic wrap until doubled.

6. Turn out onto a floured board and roll to a thickness of about ¼ inch.

7. Cut into squares or diamonds and place in a floured hotel pan and allow to double again.

8. Carefully drop into 350° peanut oil and cook until golden brown, turning once.

9. Drain on toweling and sift tons of powered sugar over them. You might give them a minute or two to cool a little—so all the powdered sugar will not be absorbed. But do not wait too long. They are wonderful while warm.

# creole calas

These are the "rice cakes" that were formerly sold in the streets of the French Quarter in the mornings. When I worked in the bakery as a teenager, we used only fresh yeast in all recipes. All recipes from that era have been converted to dry yeast here in this book. Fresh yeast just gets harder and harder to find. This recipe should make about 2 dozen.

| INGREDIENT | QUANTITY | METHOD |
|---|---|---|
| Dry yeast (this will be 1 package) | ¼ oz. | 1. Dissolve yeast in water. |
| Warm water, about 125° | ½ c. | 2. Smash the hot cooked rice with meat pounder or a potato masher. Cool the rice and place it in a stainless bowl. |
| Cooked, short grain rice | 1½ c. | |
| Large eggs, beaten | 3 | 3. Combine yeast and rice and thoroughly mix. Cover with plastic wrap and let rise in a warm place for 2 hours. |
| Sugar | ¼ c. | |
| Flour, all-purpose | 1¼ c. | |
| Salt | ½ tsp. | 4. Add eggs, sugar, flour, salt, and nutmeg to rice mixture, beating until thoroughly mixed. |
| Ground nutmeg | ¼ tsp. | |
| Peanut oil | Approx. 8 c. | 5. Heat the peanut oil in a skillet to 360°. |
| Powdered sugar | 1 c. | 6. Using a tablespoon, drop the batter into the hot oil and cook until golden brown, turning once. |
| Cinnamon, ground | 1 tbsp. | |
| | | 7. Drain well on paper toweling. Combine powdered sugar and cinnamon; sprinkle over Calas and serve immediately. |

# fresh fruit fritters

Here is another Creole morning favorite. The peach fritters are my favorite.

| INGREDIENT | QUANTITY |
|---|---|
| Flour, all-purpose | 1 c. |
| Baking powder | 1 tsp. |
| Granulated sugar | 1 tbsp. |
| Salt | ½ tsp. |
| Large eggs, separated | 2 |
| Milk | ½ c. |
| Peanut oil | 1 qt. |
| Banana pieces, sliced peaches or apples or fresh berries | About 2 lbs. |
| Powdered sugar | 1 c. |

**METHOD**

1. Sift together flour, baking powder, sugar, and salt.

2. Mix together egg yolks, milk, and 1 tablespoon peanut oil.

3. Stir into dry ingredients until well mixed. I use a wire whip for this.

4. Beat egg whites until stiff peaks form. Fold them into the batter.

5. Heat peanut oil to 360°.

6. Dip fruits in batter and fry for 3 to 4 minutes.

7. Dry on paper toweling.

8. Sprinkle fruit with powdered sugar immediately.

# pain perdu

I mention in the Red Beans and Rice (page 165) recipe that my mother did not think of cooking as something in which she wanted to get terribly involved. This dish and the Red Beans and Rice were her two best efforts. She made both quite well—and often. You probably know this as "French toast."

In France, this dish was originally known as *pain à la Romaine*, or "Roman bread," which is some indication of just how old the dish is. While the French did not conceive it, they most certainly brought it to southern Louisiana, and it was, and remains to this day, a favorite of the Creoles. *Pain perdu* means "lost bread," implying that while the bread may no longer serve as bread, it may be profitably employed in this delicious dish.

An old friend of mine, Spencer Moore, has a restaurant, Mama's Royal Café, in Cabo San Lucas, Baja, Mexico, where he serves what he calls the "World's Best French Toast"—he serves *pain perdu* and has a little rap about it. Spencer and I worked together when I had a Creole restaurant in Oakland, California, in the 1970s. His version is more luscious and elaborate (stuffed with cream cheese) than the basic recipe I offer here. The following will yield six servings.

> **LAGNIAPPE** - Several breads will work well with this recipe. Seedless challah is great—Spencer mentions this, too. Any good French or Italian bread will also give you excellent results. Thick slices are essential. The other key here is the soaking of the bread. The slices must be completely saturated with the custard mixture.

| INGREDIENT | QUANTITY |
| --- | --- |
| Large eggs, beaten | 6 |
| Milk | 1½ cups |
| Granulated sugar | ½ cup |
| Vanilla extract | 1 tbsp. |
| Nutmeg, freshly grated | To taste |
| Cinnamon, ground | ½ tsp. |
| Stale bread, thick-sliced 1¼ to 1½ inches | 12 slices |
| Butter, clarified | ½ cup |

### METHOD

1. Beat the eggs, milk, sugar, vanilla, nutmeg, and cinnamon together in a bowl large enough to dredge the slices of bread.
2. Place the slices of bread in this custard mixture and allow them to soak for at least 10 minutes.
3. Heat the clarified butter over medium heat in a fry or sauté pan or on a griddle. I like the griddle for this.
4. Sauté until golden brown on both sides.
5. Drain on toweling and hold in a warm oven (200–250°) while you sauté the remaining slices. Add additional clarified butter if needed.
6. Serve your favorite topping with the *pain*. Some Creoles sprinkle cinnamon sugar over them. Steen's cane syrup is another favorite. Maple syrup, honey, and fresh fruit with sweetened cream are a few other options.

# fruit and liqueur topping—parts list

**LAGNIAPPE** - Spencer gave me permission to share his fruit and liqueur topping with you. Here it is exactly as he wrote it.

## BANANAS

One small banana (sliced into rounds) per person sounds about right.

## PECANS

Chopped into peanut sized pieces, about a tablespoon or two per serving. Walnuts work great, taste and look just the same. I use pecans because it sounds a little fancier on the menu.

## SUGAR

A lot. I use regular granulated sugar but brown raw sugar would probably be wonderful.

## BUTTER

A lot, but you can use margarine. No one will know and margarine doesn't burn as easily as the butter.

## ORANGE LIQUEUR

Let your conscience be your guide, but I use about a half shot per serving. If you have too much money—use Grand Marnier, but any Orange liqueur will do.

## ORANGE JUICE

About half a small glass per serving.

Start the bananas frying in a hot pan with lots of butter. When the bananas start to show a little color add the sugar—enough to absorb most of the butter. Stir until the sugar has melted and add the liqueur. A word of caution here—remove the pan from the flame before you add the liqueur. The liqueur is highly flammable and it can catch fire, travel up the liqueur and set the bottle on fire. Then you're standing there looking silly with a lit Molotov cocktail in your hand. You panic and drop the bottle—the bottle breaks, spreading burning Grand Marnier across your kitchen, setting the curtains on fire, burning down your house and you get really mad at me for not warning you and I just don't need anyone else mad at me right now. If you have an electric stove you'll have to set the liqueur aflame with a cigarette lighter or a flint and rock or something. When the flame dies down add the pecans and enough orange juice to make a syrupy mix to put over your French toast. If you have a whole bunch of pretty mint growing in your back yard—a sprig of mint and some powdered sugar makes the perfect garnish. If not, an orange slice looks pretty good, too. Let me know how it turns out.

# *challah*

This is the traditional Jewish egg bread and it is always braided. It is traditionally served after *Yom Kippur* and at Jewish weddings. If you want to be traditional, sprinkle with poppy seeds instead of sesame, unless you are making it for use as Pain Perdu (see recipe page 145) in which case omit the seeds altogether.

| INGREDIENT | QUANTITY |
|---|---|
| Yeast, dry | 1½ tbsp. |
| Warm water | 2¼ c. |
| Sugar | 1 tbsp. |
| Flour, all-purpose | 6 c. |
| Salt | 2 tbsp |
| Peanut oil | 1½ tbsp. |
| Eggs, whole | 1–or 2 |
| Whole egg wash | 1 egg |
| Sesame seeds | As desired |

## METHOD

1. Combine yeast, warm water, and sugar in bowl of mixer. Allow this mixture to "work" for 5 to 10 minutes.

2. Sift flour and salt together.

3. Make the dough, using the "Straight Dough Mixing Method."

4. Remove the dough from the mixer and place in a bowl that you have coated with peanut oil. Cover the bowl with plastic wrap and permit it to double in volume in a warm place.

5. Remove ⅓ of the dough and set it aside.

6. Divide the larger piece of dough into three equal pieces.

7. Using your hands roll the three pieces into "ropes" approximately one inch thick and 14 to 16 inches long.

8. Braid these three pieces together and pinch the ends tightly.

9. Place on an oiled baking sheet, or on a sheet on which you have placed a piece of parchment paper.

10. Divide the smaller piece of dough into three equal pieces. Roll out and braid as before.

11. Place the smaller braid on top of the larger braid.

12. Paint with the egg wash and if desired sprinkle the sesame seeds over all. Allow to rise until doubled in volume.

13. Bake in a 425° oven for about 35–40 minutes.

# CREOLE VEGETABLES:
# HOW NOT TO KILL THEM

This chapter title came about from the number of times I have eaten overcooked vegetables in restaurants in the southern United States. My first real appreciation for truly fresh vegetables came at Mudd's. While the 10-acre garden did not nearly supply all the restaurant's vegetable needs, it did supply a panoply of *different* vegetables and nearly all our fresh herbs. I have had my own organic gardens whenever possible since that time. I think growing my own vegetables and herbs has given me an appreciation for keeping them as near what nature intended as possible. What I am saying is this: If you err, make it on the short side. A slightly undercooked vegetable will always be better than a slightly overcooked one.

## GREENS

Another San Francisco Bay Area restaurant that has its own garden is Greens. It has a residential Zen community, Green Gulch Farm, which provides it with fresh seasonal produce. When I was chef at Mudd's, Deborah Madison was chef at Greens. I spent a few hours in the kitchen there with her one day and was truly impressed by her respect for the produce.

# bacon-braised mustard greens

We'll begin with a "greens" vegetable from Chef Donald Link of Herbsaint. Chef Link shows great respect for this venerable southern dish and does not overcook the greens.

| INGREDIENT | QUANTITY |
|---|---|
| Mustard greens | 2–3 bunches |
| Onion, medium, diced | 1 |
| Bacon, diced | 2 c. |
| Garlic, chopped | 1 tsp. |
| Chili flakes | 1 tsp. |
| Sugar | 3 tbsp. |
| Apple cider vinegar | ½ c. |
| Chicken stock | ½ c. |
| Salt and pepper | To taste |

## METHOD

1. Start by rendering bacon in a wide rondo or pot. When bacon is halfway rendered, add onion, garlic, and chili flakes and cook until onions are soft. Add sugar, vinegar, and chicken stock.

2. Bring to a boil and add greens and cook slowly and stir often. The greens will begin to release their own liquid. Cook for about 20 minutes for larger greens and less for smaller greens. Finish with salt and pepper.

**LAGNIAPPE** - Chef Link says: Make sure to wash greens well! I usually remove the stems from the leaves and tear them into 4- or 5-inch pieces. You can cook the stems if you like, but be sure to cook them longer.

# bourbon blazed turnips

Try to find young turnips for this dish. They will be sweet and complement the bourbon perfectly.

| INGREDIENT | QUANTITY | METHOD |
|---|---|---|
| Turnips, peeled and quartered | 6–8 | 1. Dry turnips and sauté in the butter until just beginning to brown (caramelize). |
| Butter, unsalted | 4 tbsp. | |
| Marjoram | ½ tsp. | 2. Add thyme, marjoram, salt, pepper, and brown sugar and continue to sauté. |
| Thyme, whole | ½ tsp. | |
| Salt | To taste | 3. After sugar is completely dissolved and has coated the turnips, deglaze with the bourbon. |
| Pepper, black, freshly ground | To taste | |
| Brown sugar | 2 tbsp. | 4. Add stock, cover, and bake for about 20 to 25 minutes in a 375° oven. |
| Bourbon | 1 oz. | |
| Stock, chicken or brown | 6 oz. | |

# aubergines à la provençale

This is a French Creole dish brought over by early immigrants.

| INGREDIENT | QUANTITY |
|---|---|
| Eggplant, small, if possible | 3–4 |
| Lemon juice | 2 tbsp. |
| Salt | 1 tbsp. |
| Tomatoes, peeled, seeded, diced | 1–2 c. |
| Olive oil, extra virgin | ¼ c. |
| Garlic, minced | 1 tbsp. |
| Pesto | 1 tbsp. |
| Parsley, minced | 2 tbsp. |
| Pepper, black, freshly ground | To taste |

**METHOD**

1. Cut eggplant in half lengthwise.

2. Sprinkle a little salt and spread a little of the lemon juice over the cut halves.

3. Bake in a 450° oven for 10 minutes.

4. Remove from oven and cool slightly. Carefully scoop out the flesh, leaving ¾ in. on all sides. Dice flesh.

5. Sweat eggplant and tomatoes in olive oil.

6. Add garlic and pesto and continue to sweat.

7. Add parsley and remainder of lemon juice.

8. Add salt and pepper to taste.

9. Fill hollowed eggplant halves with mixture, and bake in a 450° oven for 10 minutes.

# pesto

| INGREDIENT | QUANTITY |
|---|---|
| Fresh basil leaves, stems removed | 4 oz. |
| Pine nuts | ½ c. |
| Garlic cloves | 6 |
| Pepper, black freshly ground | To taste |
| Olive oil, extra virgin | ½ c. |
| Parmesan cheese, freshly grated | ⅔ c. |
| Salt | To taste |

## METHOD

1. Place basil, pine nuts, garlic, and pepper in food processor.

2. Turn on processor and add oil in a thin stream. Process until a purée has been obtained.

3. Remove mixture from food processor and combine with cheese in a mixing bowl. Taste before adding salt, as some Parmesans are quite salty.

4. This stores quite well in the refrigerator. Make at least the quantity listed above. You'll regret not having it if you make too little.

# melanzane alla parmigiana

I think you will find this version of this Italian classic much lighter than the fare found in many Italian/Creole restaurants. The eggplant is not "battered" here.

| INGREDIENT | QUANTITY | METHOD |
|---|---|---|
| Eggplant, fried | 4 | 1. Fry the eggplant. |
| Roma Tomatoes, diced | 1 qt. | 2. Mix the tomatoes, garlic, and parsley. |
| Garlic, minced | 1 tbsp. | 3. Place a thin layer of the tomato mixture over the eggplant. |
| Parsley, minced | ½ c. | |
| Salt | To taste | 4. Salt and pepper the eggplant. Sprinkle a little oregano over. |
| Pepper, black, freshly ground | To taste | |
| Mozzarella, grated | 2 c. | 5. Place a layer of the cheeses over the tomatoes. |
| Parmesan, grated | 1 c. | 6. Continue with layers until you have exhausted the eggplant. |
| Oregano, whole | 1 tbsp. | |
| Butter, unsalted | 2 tbsp. | 7. Finish with eggplant with a little Parmesan sprinkled over the top. Dot with butter and bake at 425° for about 30 minutes. (You may need to skim some fat and/or water from the dish while it is baking.) Allow the dish to "set up" for 5 or 10 minutes before serving. |

**FRIED EGGPLANT** - Peel eggplant and slice into disks about ½ in. thick. Salt eggplant and let it drain in a colander for about 30 minutes. Dry thoroughly. Fry in 350° peanut or olive oil until golden brown. Drain well.

# boiled artichokes

This is the easiest artichoke preparation. And there is absolutely no shame in serving this vegetable prepared in the simplest manner. They are delicious alone with just the lemon butter or with hollandaise sauce (see page 16).

**LAGNIAPPE** - You may well wonder why artichokes are featured in so many New Orleans restaurants since California accounts for 100% of the commercial artichoke production in the United States.

Time for a little history. French immigrants brought artichokes with them when they settled the Louisiana Territory around the middle of the 18th century. They were widely grown in Louisiana until World War II. So, we had about 200 years of artichoke history in New Orleans. Production never resumed after the war.

| INGREDIENT | QUANTITY |
|---|---|
| Artichokes | 6–8 |
| Boiling water | 2 gal. |
| Salt | 1 tbsp. |
| Lemon | 1 |

## METHOD

1. Using scissors, cut the sharp points off the tips of the artichoke's leaves. Rub all cut areas immediately with a half lemon to prevent oxidation. Place salt in boiling water.

2. Cut the bottom stem off flush with the artichoke bottom. Rub cut end with lemon.

3. Gently pry the artichoke open to expose the small leaves in the center. Pull them out.

4. Using either a strong spoon or a melon baller, cut the choke out of the center of the artichoke. Squeeze lemon down inside the artichoke.

5. Place the artichokes in boiling water. Cover them with either a cloth kitchen towel or cheesecloth. Squeeze the remaining juice from the lemon and place it in the water with the artichokes.

6. Boil until a knife inserted in the base of the artichoke goes in easily. For most artichokes, this boiling period will last 25 to 40 minutes.

**LAGNIAPPE** - If serving the artichokes hot, we like them with either a lemon butter or a hollandaise sauce. If served cold, we accompany them with a garlic or a seasoned mayonnaise.

# stuffed artichokes

I think the Italian influence is quite obvious in this dish, but it is not Italian. It is a true New Orleans Creole dish—born and "breaded" here. My daddy would stop on his way home from work in New Orleans and pick up a dish very much like this one at Manale's.

These stuffed artichokes are a staple on the altars constructed for St. Joseph's Day (March 19) by those of Italian extraction in New Orleans.

| INGREDIENT | QUANTITY |
|---|---|
| Artichokes, medium, trimmed, choke removed | 6–8 |
| Bread crumbs, French | 3 c. |
| Parmesan, freshly grated | 1½ c. |
| Anchovies, finely minced | 1¾ oz. |
| Parsley, finely minced | ¼ c. |
| Cayenne | 1 tsp. |
| Thyme, whole, minced | 1 tbsp. |
| Olive oil, extra virgin | 6 oz. |
| Lemon juice | 2 tbsp. |
| Salt | To taste |
| Pepper, black, freshly ground | To taste |

## METHOD

1. Rub artichokes with a cut lemon and hold in water acidulated with lemon juice until ready to cook.

2. Combine all other ingredients except olive oil and lemon juice in a bowl.

3. Add half the olive oil to bread crumb mixture and work in thoroughly.

4. Drain artichokes and loosely stuff the leaves and center with the bread crumb mixture.

5. Squeeze lemon juice over artichokes and drizzle remaining olive oil over them.

6. Pack artichokes close together in a brazier and pour in about 1 inch of the acidulated water.

7. Bring to boil, reduce to simmer, and cook, covered, for 30 to 40 minutes or until a knife inserted in the base goes in smoothly.

# mirliton ratatouille

**LAGNIAPPE** - Now this may be a vegetable you may not be able to obtain in your local supermarket. Mirliton is Creole French for a tropical squash, pale green in color, that you may know as chayote or vegetable pear. In the original French, mirliton is a reed flute and, later, a pastry named for its shape.

| INGREDIENT | QUANTITY |
|---|---|
| Mirlitons | 3 lb. |
| Eggplant, medium | 1 |
| Onions, yellow, medium | 2 |
| Bell peppers, green, medium | 2 |
| Bell peppers, red, medium | 2 |
| Roma tomatoes , fresh or canned, peeled, seeded, and diced | 3 c. |
| Garlic, minced | 2 tbsp. |
| Olive oil, extra virgin | ¾ c. |
| Flat leaf Italian parsley, minced | ½ c. |
| Bay leaves | 2 |
| Thyme, fresh | 1 tbsp. |
| Sea salt and freshly ground black pepper | To taste |

## METHOD

1. Cut the mirlitons in half and remove the seed.

2. Slice into ½-inch slices. Peel the eggplant and slice, lengthwise, into ½-inch slices.

3. Slice the onions in half lengthwise. Then slice the halves across the grain into ¼-inch slices.

4. Quarter the peppers lengthwise and remove the white membranes and seeds. Cut into a short julienne. Mince the garlic.

5. Brush the mirliton and eggplant slices with olive oil and grill until about half cooked and nicely grill-marked with diamond-shaped grill marks.

6. Sauté the onions and peppers in the remaining olive oil until half cooked. Add the garlic, and sauté for 1 additional minute. Add Roma tomatoes and all herbs and spices and warm through.

7. Oil a casserole and alternate layers of grilled mirliton with onion and pepper mixture, then a layer of grilled eggplant, then onion and pepper again. Continue until all ingredients are in casserole. Drizzle a little olive oil over the top and bake at 350° for 30 minutes.

# baked creole eggplant delmonico's restaurant

Let's wrap up our vegetable chapter with a few eggplant dishes. Creoles have been cooking this versatile vegetable since their arrival in Louisiana. This is my version of a recipe that was once served at Delmonico's.

| INGREDIENT | QUANTITY |
|---|---|
| Medium eggplants, diced | 2 |
| Onion, diced | 1 c. |
| Raw peeled shrimp | 1 c. |
| Celery, diced | ¾ c. |
| Butter, unsalted | ½ c. |
| Dry rub (see page 48) | To taste |
| Salt and freshly ground black pepper | To taste |
| Breadcrumbs | ½ c. |

## METHOD

1. Slice eggplant in half lengthwise and salt. Bake in a 350° oven for about 25 minutes. Peel eggplant and dice into ¾ in. cubes.

2. Sauté onion, chopped shrimp, and celery in butter. Add dry rub and salt and pepper.

   Add eggplant. Put in a buttered baking dish and sprinkle with bread crumbs. Bake in a 425° oven for an additional 20 minutes.

# french fried eggplant
## styled after a galatoire's recipe

Are you ready for this—eggplant and powdered sugar? Serves 6.

| INGREDIENT | QUANTITY | METHOD |
|---|---|---|
| Eggplant, peeled and sliced into ¾ in. strips | 3 small | 1. Soak eggplant 30 minutes in salted water. |
| Eggs, large | 3 | 2. Rinse and pat dry. |
| Milk | 1½ c. | 3. Make a batter with egg and milk and season well with salt and pepper. |
| Flour, all-purpose | 1 c. | 4. Dip eggplant into batter, roll in flour and deep-fry until golden. |
| Salt and white pepper | To taste | 5. Sprinkle with additional salt and serve with powdered sugar. |
| Peanut oil for deep frying | 2 qt. | |
| Powdered sugar, sifted | 1 c. | |

# stuffed eggplant

This is my version of an eggplant dish I know was served at one time at the Bon Ton Café on Magazine. The Bon Ton, a New Orleans tradition, is known principally for the starched white uniforms worn by the waitresses and the bread pudding.

| INGREDIENT | QUANTITY |
|---|---|
| Eggplant, small, cut in half | 3–4 |
| Extra virgin olive oil | ¼ c. |
| Bell peppers, medium, diced | 2–3 |
| Onions, medium, diced | 2 c. |
| Parsley, minced | ½ c. |
| Celery, diced | ½ c. |
| Garlic cloves, minced | 3 or 4 |
| Shrimp, medium, peeled and deveined | ½ lb. |
| White lump crabmeat | ½ lb. |
| Salt and pepper | To taste |
| Bread crumbs | 1 c. |
| Paprika | Few dashes |
| Butter, unsalted, softened | 4 oz. |

## METHOD

1. Bake eggplant in a 375° oven for about 20 minutes. Scoop out flesh and dice. Reserve eggplant "cases."

2. Sauté bell peppers, onion, celery, and garlic together until translucent. Add eggplant.

3. Sauté on medium heat until most water is cooked out, then add the shrimp. Cook for another 5 minutes.

4. Remove from pan and mix in crabmeat, parsley, salt and pepper in a large stainless bowl. Add bread crumbs. Stuff eggplant cases and place on an oiled sheet pan.

5. Sprinkle some bread crumbs on top and a few dashes of paprika. Dot with butter. Bake until done or browned in 350°F oven—about 25 to 30 minutes.

# stuffed bell peppers creole style

Okay, so I fudged a little when I said my mother only made two dishes (Red Beans and Rice and Pain Perdu). She made this Creole standby, too. Notice you will need seven green bell peppers for this dish. Read the entire recipe. Serves 6.

| INGREDIENT | QUANTITY |
|---|---|
| Large green bell peppers | 6 |
| Ground chuck | 1½ lb. |
| Extra virgin olive oil | ¼ c. |
| Onion, minced | ¼ c. |
| Celery, diced | ½ c. |
| Green bell pepper, diced | ½ c. |
| Jalapeño, minced | 1 or 2 |
| Salt | To taste |
| Pepper, black, freshly ground | To taste |
| Cooked long grain rice | 2 c. |

## METHOD

1. Remove stem and just enough of the top so you can get inside and cut out the white membranes and remove the seeds from the peppers.

2. Cover peppers with boiling water. Cook, uncovered, for 5 minutes; drain upside and set aside.

3. Sauté the ground chuck until caramelized and drain in a sieve.

4. Using the same fat, cook the celery, onions, and both the jalepeño and the diced green bell peppers. Drain.

5. Add salt, pepper, and cooked rice; mix well.

6. Fill peppers with this mixture.

7. Place the peppers in an oiled baking dish and nap with Creole Sauce—be liberal.

8. Bake, covered, at 350° for 30 minutes.

9. Uncover and bake 15 minutes more.

   Serve with Creole Sauce (see page 23).

# chapter 9

## STARCHES, HEAVY AND LIGHT

This is a short chapter, partly because the range of side-dish starches that will complement a main course and not dominate the plate is fairly short. Also, several starches are scattered throughout the book—Anne Kearney's "Dirty Rice," for instance.

# oyster dressing

We will begin our chapter on starches with an old Creole favorite—Oyster Dressing. This is my all-purpose oyster dressing. You may serve this as a side dish with sautéed or fried seafood or you may stuff game or fowl with it.

| INGREDIENT | QUANTITY | METHOD |
|---|---|---|
| Butter, unsalted | ¼ lb. | 1. Melt the butter over medium heat. |
| Onions, medium, yellow, finely chopped | 2 | 2. Sauté the onions, celery, green onions, and garlic until translucent, stirring frequently. |
| Celery, finely chopped | 1 c. | 3. Gradually add the chopped oysters. Cook about 4 minutes, constantly stirring. Add the parsley; stir. |
| Green onions, thinly sliced | 1 c. | |
| Garlic, minced | 1½ tbsp. | 4. Lower the heat and simmer for 5 minutes. Add the cheese and pepper; stir. |
| Oysters, roughly chopped (Reserve oyster liquor to be added later) | 4 dozen | 5. Remove from the heat and begin stirring in the croutons a little at a time. |
| Parsley, finely chopped | ½ c. | 6. Add the pecans and oyster liquor and stir. |
| Freshly ground black pepper | To taste | 7. To serve as a stand-alone casserole, bake in a buttered casserole dish in a 350° oven for about 20 minutes. |
| Peccorino Romano or Parmigiano, grated | ¾ c. | |
| Garlic croutons | 3 c. | |
| Oyster liquor | 1½ c. | |
| Pecans, chopped | ¾ c. | |

**GARLIC CROUTONS:** Take a loaf of aging French bread and trim off the crust. Cut the bread into ¾ in. cubes. Heat ¼ cup of extra virgin olive oil in a sauté pan. Add 2 tbsp. of minced garlic. When the first bits of garlic begin to turn brown pour the oil through a sieve and remove the solid pieces of garlic. Cool the oil slightly. Toss the croutons in a bowl with the oil and salt and pepper to taste. Spread the croutons on a sheet pan and bake in a 450° oven for 10 minutes. Use these in salads, soups, and dressings. Hide them. They will magically evaporate otherwise.

# rice pilaf

Notice I am using "converted" rice in this recipe. This is a rice that has been parboiled and partially cooked. Do not confuse it with "minute rice." The advantage of converted rice is twofold: a slightly reduced cooking time, and, since converted rice is not starchy, there is virtually no likelihood of the rice being sticky. The grains will remain completely separate. You may use any long- or short-grain rice you prefer as long as you adjust the cooking time appropriately.

| INGREDIENT | QUANTITY | METHOD |
|---|---|---|
| Butter, unsalted | 4 tbsp. | 1. Melt butter over medium heat in a saucepan. |
| Onion, yellow, finely minced | ½ c. | 2. Sweat onion, carrots, and celery until just soft. |
| Celery, finely minced | ½ c. | 3. Add garlic and ginger. |
| Carrot, finely minced | ½ c. | 4. Add rice and toss until rice is completely coated with the butter. |
| Garlic, minced | 1 tbsp. | |
| Ginger, fresh, minced | 1 tsp. | 5. Add stock, salt, pepper, and turmeric and thoroughly incorporate. |
| Rice, converted | 2¼ c. | |
| Chicken stock | 2 c. | 6. Cover pot and simmer over very low heat for about 15 minutes or until liquid is completely absorbed. |
| Dry white wine | ¼ c. | |
| Lemon juice | 2 tbsp. | |
| Salt | To taste | |
| Pepper | To taste | |
| Turmeric | 1 tbsp. | |

# risotto milanese

Risotto Milanese dates back to 1574, when a stained-glass artisan named Zafferano added some saffron that he used for coloring his paints to his risotto for his daughter's wedding. In no time, this dish was the talk of the town and still is—or so the story goes. Saffron is the world's most expensive spice. It comes from small purple crocus flowers that produce three stigmas per flower that are handpicked and dried. It takes 14,000 of these stigmas to produce 1 ounce of saffron. You really must use the arborio rice for a successful risotto. And stay there while you are cooking it!

| INGREDIENT | QUANTITY |
|---|---|
| Chicken stock | 7 c. |
| Saffron threads (or powdered saffron ⅛ tsp.) | 4–6 |
| Olive oil, extra virgin | ¼ c. |
| Onions, yellow, minced | ¾ c. |
| Arborio rice | 2 c. |
| Unsalted butter | 2 tbsp. |
| Salt and pepper | To taste |
| Dry white wine | ½ c. |
| Parmesan, grated | 1 c. |

## METHOD

1. In a large pot, heat the stock but don't let it come to a boil. Just let it simmer.

2. Heat the oil in a separate heavy-bottomed pot over medium heat.

3. Add the onion and cook slowly until translucent.

4. Stir in the rice until the grains of rice are coated with the oil. This will keep them from sticking together.

5. Cook for a couple of minutes until the rice gives off a nutty smell.

6. Start by adding 1 cup of hot stock, stirring continuously.

7. As the rice absorbs the stock, begin adding ½ cup of stock at a time, stirring continuously until all the stock is used (15–20 minutes).

8. Remove from heat and stir in the wine and saffron.

# haricot rouge et riz

Every dish has a story. In New Orleans, Monday was traditionally wash day. Supposedly, the woman of the house would put a pot of beans on the stove to cook all day while she took care of the family's quotidian necessities. Often this dish is served as a side dish. My version is a full-blown main course. I tell my students that if you are consuming red beans and run across potatoes in your fork or spoon, it is probably my mother's version channeled through me. Or, it has at least traversed the length of the Irish Channel in New Orleans.

My mother, God rest her soul, was not the world's greatest cook. This came about more from disinclination than from any lack of ability. Also, she was a working woman. However, she did prepare one truly wonderful dish: Red Beans and Rice. In New Orleans, it is traditional to eat this dish on Monday. We had it just about every Monday when I was a child. My version is "after" hers. I doubt that one will find another version as laden with meats as this one.

## INGREDIENT

| INGREDIENT | QUANTITY |
|---|---|
| Red beans, boiled and "soaked" for 1 hour (see note) | 1 lb. |
| Water | 3 qt. |
| Ham hocks | 1 lb. |
| Onions, yellow, thinly sliced | 2 c. |
| Bell pepper, thin julienne | 2 c. |
| Garlic, minced | 1 tbsp. |
| Celery, sliced thinly on the bias | 2 c. |
| Ham, julienne | 1 c. |
| Sausage, hot (andouille, for example) | 2 or 3 |
| Cumin | 1 tsp. |
| Pepper, black, freshly ground | 1 tsp. |
| Pepper, cayenne | 1 tsp. |
| Bay leaves | 4 |
| Thyme, whole | 1 tbsp. |
| Tomatoes, peeled, seeded, chopped | 2 c. |
| Tomato purée | ½ c. |
| Potatoes, ½-inch dice | 3 c. |
| Salt | To taste |
| Parsley, minced | ¼ c. |

## METHOD

1. Drain beans and place in a pot with the water, ham hocks, onions, bell pepper, garlic, celery, ham, sausage (sliced), cumin, peppers, bay leaf, thyme, tomatoes, purée, potatoes, salt, and parsley.
2. Bring the pot to a boil, reduce to a simmer, then cover and simmer for approximately 1 hour. Check the beans, and if they are not yet soft, cook until they are.
3. Remove ham hock from pot and cut meat off the bone and dice. Return to pot.
4. We like to make our boiled rice separate and serve the red beans in a soup bowl over the rice.

**LAGNIAPPE** - I call this the "bean trick." We use it quite a bit with dried legumes. Bring the beans to a rolling boil in ample water. Boil them for about 5 minutes. Place a lid on the pot and allow them to soak for at least an hour.

The beans (peas, lentils, etc.) will have reconstituted as if you had soaked them in cold water overnight. This speeds up the process quite a bit. We follow this procedure for all our bean soups and purées as well.

# purée of garlic potatoes

The thick-skinned Burbank-type Idaho potatoes are best for making this more or less traditional American dish. I serve this with the Poulet Sauté, but it also goes very well with roast pork, beef stews, and nearly all hearty dishes.

| INGREDIENT | QUANTITY | METHOD |
|---|---|---|
| Boiling water | To cover | 1. Place potatoes in boiling water with 1 teaspoon of salt. |
| Potatoes, baking, medium, peeled cut into large pieces | 6 | 2. Boil until potatoes are just tender. |
| Garlic, finely minced | 1 tbsp. | 3. Sweat the garlic in a little of the butter. *Do not allow the garlic to brown.* Add to potatoes. |
| Salt | To taste | 4. Put potatoes and garlic through food mill. Add salt and pepper. |
| Pepper, white | To taste | |
| Milk | 1½ c. | 5. Add milk and thoroughly combine with a whip or a wooden spoon. |
| Butter, unsalted | 2 tbsp. | 6. Add and thoroughly incorporate butter. |
| | | 7. Place in a large pastry bag equipped with a large star tube. |
| | | 8. Pipe potatoes into center of plate and arrange your food (the Poulet Sauté with Wild Mushrooms, for instance; see page 110) around them. |

# patates douces et panais frites
# (fried sweet potatoes and parsnips)

Although this dish could easily have been placed in the vegetable chapter we tend to treat both sweet potatoes and parsnips as starches in the ways we use them. Traditionally, if it were small enough to get it into a pot, a Creole would fry it. Try these as a side dish with sautéed meats. Some Creoles served them with sugar as a sweet. Try them this savory way. Serves 6.

| INGREDIENTS | QUANTITY |
|---|---|
| Sweet potatoes, medium | 2–3 |
| Parsnips | 4–6 |
| Boiling water, salted | 2 qt. |
| Peanut oil | 2 qt. |
| Kosher salt | To taste |
| Pepper, black, freshly ground | To taste |

### METHOD

1. Boil the sweet potatoes and parsnips until they are just tender—a paring knife will easily pierce them.

2. Drain, cool, and peel. Refrigerate them for an hour or so to firm them.

3. Heat the peanut oil to 360°.

4. Slice potatoes and parsnips into a ½ inch julienne.

5. Fry until golden brown. Drain and salt and pepper immediately.

# GRITS

Creoles are pretty gritty folk. I remember one particular breakfast at my father's house. In attendance were my father, my stepmother, and my Aunt Maye and I. My stepmother, Jimmie (yes), and my Aunt Maye did the cooking. My father and I sat at the kitchen table and watched. They made sausage, bacon, ham, eggs, biscuits, coffee, fresh-squeezed orange juice, and, of course, grits. For many New Orleanians a breakfast without grits is like a day without rain—unheard of in other words.

Just what is a grit?

First, let's take care of the word origin. The word "grits" comes from the Anglo-Saxon (Old English) word "grytt," for "bran" or "something ground." We have been using the term "grits" to mean this particular ground corn dish since at least the 18th century.

Grits are hominy made from flint or dent corn, varieties with hard kernels that are dried on the cob then removed and soaked in a solution of baking soda, lime, or wood ash (lye). After the kernels get soft they swell. Next, they are hulled, degermed, dried, and ground. Usually grits are made from white corn, although you will see some yellow grits. Masa harina, the flour used to make corn tortillas, is processed in much the same manner. I do not want to get into the science here, but this process actually makes some of the nutrients in corn more accessible to our bodies. Stone ground grits are the more natural product and will take longer to cook since they contain the germ. Grits are a cereal, folks.

First we'll tackle my basic cheese grits recipe and then I'll give you a couple of other things to do with them.

# cheese grits

Serves 8 to 10.

| INGREDIENT | QUANTITY |
|---|---|
| Skim milk | 6 c. |
| Salt | 2 tsp. |
| Freshly ground white pepper | 1 tsp. |
| Unsalted butter | 4 tbsp. |
| White grits | 1¼ c. |
| Parmigiano Reggiano, grated | ½ c. |
| Provolone, grated | ½ c. |
| Sharp cheddar, grated | ½ c. |

## METHOD

1. Over medium heat, in a saucepan bring the milk, salt, pepper, and butter to a boil. Watch the pot! It will boil over if you space out.

2. Slowly stir in the grits.

3. Add the cheeses a little at a time. Check seasoning.

4. Serve with any breakfast or brunch dish—always with Grillades (see page 121). Do not worry about leftovers. I have a couple of things you can do with them.

**LAGNIAPPE** - The above quantities are for a package that simply says "Grits" on the label (cooking time about 20 minutes). If you are using "Quick Grits" (cooking time five minutes) you will need about 25% less liquid. If you are using "Stone Ground Grits" (cooking time 35 to 40 minutes) you will need a little more liquid. Read the package, folks.

Hey, it's Southern food, folks, somebody is going to figure out a way to fry it. Might as well be me.

| INGREDIENT | QUANTITY |
|---|---|
| Grits, cooked | 2 c. |
| Chicken stock (see page 11) | 1 c. |
| Milk, whole | ¾ c. |
| Baking powder | ½ tsp. |
| All-purpose flour | 1 tbsp. |
| Eggs, beaten | 2 |
| Pepper, freshly ground | To taste |
| Butter, unsalted | ½ c. |
| Eggs, beaten | 3 |
| Extra virgin olive oil | 2 c. |

### METHOD

1. Place grits, stock, and ½ cup of the milk in a saucepan over low heat. Add the baking powder. Warm through.

2. Stir in flour, eggs, pepper, and butter. Cook until butter melts.

3. Butter a ½ sheet pan and spread the mixture evenly over the pan—to a depth of about one inch. Refrigerate for at least 1 hour.

4. Using a round cookie cutter cut out circles no more than 2½ inches.

5. Mix the 3 beaten eggs and remaining milk together.

6. Dip in the egg batter and sauté in the olive oil until golden brown. Drain.

# souffléd grits

Serve as a side dish with hearty meat dishes such as roasts and stews. This will remind some of your guests of polenta. It should, they are closely related.

This is a fairly elegant manner in which you may use your leftover grits.

| INGREDIENT | QUANTITY |
|---|---|
| Cooked cheese grits | 4 c. |
| Eggs, large, separated | 4 |
| Green onions, whites only | ½ c. |
| Tabasco | Dash |
| Worcestershire | Dash |
| Parmigiano Reggiano | ½ c. |
| Unsalted butter, softened | ¼ c. |
| Tasso, diced | ½ c. |

**METHOD**

1. Warm the grits (not too hot). Beat in the egg yolks.

2. Whip the egg whites until fairly stiff peaks form. Butter soufflé dishes or individual soufflé ramekins and place some of the Parmesan in each. Roll the dishes around until the cheese coats the inside completely. Knock out excess.

3. Add the onions and Tasso to the mixture off heat.

4. Gently fold in the beaten egg whites. Fill soufflé dishes ¾ full with the mixture.

5. Bake in a 350° oven for about 20 minutes or until soufflés are puffed and browned on top. Check for doneness with a piece of dried spaghetti. If it comes out clean, they are done. Serve immediately.

## *chapter 10*

# DESSERTS, SWEETS, AND TREATS

Many restaurants nowadays make the mistake of serving heavy desserts, items that were once meant to be midmorning, late-night, or afternoon snacks. The desserts featured here are intended to be light after-dinner complements to the meal. If you serve one of the heavier sweets, lighten the load by cutting the portion sizes. The bread pudding recipes and the Baked Alaska (page 190) show well in small portions.

Although my focus is usually pointed at the courses preceding dessert, these few that follow fall well within reasonable cooking-skill *and* consumption parameters. The Creole desserts I remember from my youth were well-thought-out ends to wonderful meals. This version of a true French classic by John Harris fits the classic dessert concept.

# apple tarte tatin with caramel sauce and vanilla ice cream

Here is Chef John Harris of Lilette's version of the French Tart Tatin. I particularly like the sour cream dough. Makes 4–6 servings (with dough left over).

| INGREDIENT | QUANTITY |
|---|---|
| **SOUR CREAM DOUGH** | |
| Flour, all-purpose | 1¼ lb. |
| Salt | ½ tsp. |
| Unsalted butter | 15 oz. |
| Sour cream | 9 oz. |
| **TATIN** | |
| Granny Smith apples peeled, cored, and cut in half vertically | 6 |
| Butter, unsalted | 1 stick |
| Granulated sugar | ⅔ c. |
| **CARAMEL SAUCE** | |
| Granulated sugar | 1 c. |
| Water | 2 tbsp. |
| Honey | 1 tbsp. |
| Butter, unsalted | 2 oz. |
| Heavy cream | 2 oz. |

## TART TATIN PREPARATION INSTRUCTIONS

1. *To prepare dough:* In Kitchen Aid–type mixer, using a paddle, mix flour and salt for 10 seconds. Dice cold butter and mix for 15 seconds. Turn mixer off, mush butter pieces with fingers. Add sour cream and mix until dough comes together in a ball. Turn onto floured surface and knead briefly until together. Cut into 4-ounce balls and roll into 8-inch pieces. Freeze leftover dough in between wax paper for future use.

2. *To prepare caramel sauce:* In small pot, boil water, sugar, and honey rapidly. The sugar will begin to turn a deep brown. Turn off flame and let sit for 2 minutes. Wisk in butter and cream until smooth. Reserve. May be kept out for up to 1 week.

3. *To prepare the tatin:* Melt butter in 7-inch nonstick skillet. Add sugar and cook on high until deep brown (about 5 minutes). Turn flame to low, arrange apples in circular pattern all the way around, and place 2 pieces in center. Cook on low heat for about 8 minutes. Place in 375° oven for about 45 minutes or until apples are tender. Place 1 piece of rolled-out dough onto apples and finish baking for another 15 minutes until dough is golden brown. Let tart cool for 30 minutes. Place a large plate over the top of the pan, turn pan over, and pop tart out onto the plate.

4. *To serve:* Slice wedges of tatin, place on plate with 1 scoop of vanilla ice cream, and drizzle with caramel sauce.

# gateau de roi (twelfth night king cake)

What can I say about the king cake? First, it is not a cake—it is a "coffee cake." Traditionally in New Orleans, the first king cakes are served on January 6. For those of you not familiar with canonical goings-on, January 6 is the Twelfth Night (or the twelfth day of Christmas). So, what's so significant about this day? The Magi dropped in on the stable on this evening, bearing gifts. Some other names for Twelfth Night: "Epiphany," "Little Christmas," and "King's Day"—beginning to get the idea? The other significant thing about this cake is the fact that serving it marks the beginning of carnival in New Orleans: To all you non–New Orleanians out there, Mardi Gras.

There are lots of individual traditions in New Orleans involving this brioche or coffeecake. The first day of Epiphany, January 6, sees the emergence of the first king cakes of the season.

You might see (or, rather, not see) plastic babies hidden in most of the cakes—to represent the Christ child, obviously. I do remember going to school with my Aunt Maye when I was about 5 years old and finding a pecan—in the shell—instead of the baby. She rigged it so I got the pecan. So I got to be king for a day.

The tradition says, though, whoever gets the "prize" must either bring a cake to the next party or host the next party. These cakes are made throughout the carnival season until Mardi Gras or Fat Tuesday, the last day before the beginning of Lent, Ash Wednesday—during which *all* New Orleanians wear sackcloth and sit in dirt and ashes. Yeah, right.

When I make this cake for my classes, I just lay the baby out on top to avoid a "Culinary Student Chokes on Plastic Baby" headline the next morning. Remember, if you gag a loved one or friend, Chef Carey warned you.

All that stuff being said, this may well be the world's ugliest cake. I have absolutely no problem with that. The cake derives its appearance from the colored sugars with which it is festooned. The "official" Mardi Gras—and king cake—colors are purple, green, and gold. These colors are both the Mardi Gras colors and the colors of Rex, the king of Mardi Gras. The colors were supposedly selected by Rex in 1892, 20 years after the founding of the Krewe of Rex, to represent, respectively, justice, faith, and power.

## INGREDIENT    QUANTITY

### DOUGH

| Ingredient | Quantity |
|---|---|
| Water, warm | ¾ c. |
| Yeast, dried | 1½ oz. |
| Milk, scalded and cooled | ¾ c. |
| Flour, all-purpose | 6½ c. |
| Eggs, large | 3 |
| Butter, unsalted, melted | ¼ lb. |
| Lemon zest | 1 tbsp. |
| Orange zest | 1 tbsp. |

### FILLING

| Ingredient | Quantity |
|---|---|
| Butter, unsalted, softened | ½ c. |
| Powdered sugar | 1¼ c. |
| Dark brown sugar | ½ c. |
| Cinnamon, ground | 3 tbsp. |
| Pecans, chopped | 1 c. |
| Cream cheese | ½ lb. |

### ICING

| Ingredient | Quantity |
|---|---|
| Powdered sugar, sifted | 3 c. |
| Butter, unsalted, melted | ¾ c. |
| Vanilla extract | 1½ tbsp. |
| Hot water | 2–3 tbsp. |

## METHOD

### DOUGH

1. Combine water, dry yeast, and milk in mixer bowl. Water and milk should not be over 130°. Allow mixture to "work" for a few minutes.
2. Slowly add flour, 1 cup at a time.
3. When nearly all the flour has been added, add the eggs, one at a time.
4. Slowly pour in melted butter with mixer running all the while.
5. Add zests.
6. Set aside in a buttered bowl to rise while you make the filling and the icing.

### FILLING

1. Cream all ingredients together in mixer. Set aside.

### ICING

1. Combine first three ingredients in a bowl and add hot water until you have a viscous consistency that will just barely pour.

### MAKING THE CAKE

1. Divide the dough into three equal balls.
2. Using a rolling pin, roll each piece of dough into a strip about 2½ feet long and 5 or 6 inches wide.
3. Spread the filling down the center of each piece of dough.
4. Fold over the sides of the dough strips and form a cylinder of each. Try to keep the filling inside.
5. Braid the three strips together, form into an oval, and pinch the ends together.
6. Carefully lift onto a sheet pan.
7. Allow the cake to double in size.
8. Bake in a 375° oven for about 35 minutes.

## FINISHING THE CAKE

Place an icing or cooling rack on another sheet pan and remove the cake to it. Allow the cake to come to room temperature. This is a good time to make the icing above.

You will now need three colored sanding sugars. I use yellow, green, and lavender.

Pour the icing over the cake, covering it completely. Don't worry—some will run off. Sprinkle the three sugars over the top of the cake, forming a wide band of each color.

If you have any Mardi Gras trinkets, such as doubloons or beads, lying around, drape them decoratively over and around the cake. If you plan to serve the cake to sober, attentive people who will pay attention when you tell them there is a plastic baby inside, hide the baby.

# creole cream cheese cheesecake

When I was 13 or 14 I used to meet my Aunt Maye downtown "under the clock." Let me explain. The clock was on the D.H. Holmes department store on Canal. Simply put, it was where you met people downtown. Aunt Maye would take me into the restaurant inside the store where she touted the cheesecake to me. It was very good. Hell, I don't know if they made or bought it. It does form one of my fond food memories, though. The department store sadly departed in 1989. If you are set on making a real Creole cheesecake you will need to plan a day or two ahead.

## INGREDIENT / QUANTITY

### THE CRUST

| Ingredient | Quantity |
| --- | --- |
| Graham cracker crumbs | 1½ c. |
| Granulated sugar | ¼ c. |
| Butter, unsalted, melted | 4 tbsp. |

### THE CHEESECAKE

| Ingredient | Quantity |
| --- | --- |
| Creole cream cheese | 24 oz. |
| Philadelphia cream cheese | 16 oz. |
| Sugar, granulated | 1½ c. |
| Vanilla extract | 2 tbsp. |
| Lemon zest | 2 tbsp. |
| Large eggs | 3 |

## METHOD

### THE CRUST

1. Thoroughly combine graham cracker crumbs and sugar.
2. Slowly add butter and mix.
3. Press the mixture into a buttered 10-inch spring form pan.
4. Refrigerate for about an hour.

### THE CHEESECAKE

1. Preheat your oven to 350°.
2. Soften both cheeses and then place in a mixer with the paddle attachment.
3. Cream the cheeses together and slowly add the sugar, vanilla, and zest.
4. Add eggs, one at a time completely incorporating each before adding the next.
5. Remove the shell from the refrigerator and fold the cheese mixture into it. Lift the pan and tap it gently on the counter to level the filling.
6. Bake in the center of the oven for about one hour. The cake should have begun to brown around the edges and will be slightly gelatinous in the very center.
7. Cool the cheesecake very slowly. This is essential to prevent cracking. Do this on a cooling rack.
8. Turn your oven up to 425°.

*continued*

**LAGNIAPPE** - Creole cream cheese is very different from the cream cheeses available in supermarkets across the country. You will find it more like a firm sour cream than cream cheese. I only know of one dairy currently manufacturing Creole Cream cheese for wide distribution—the Bittersweet Plantation Dairy, an operation put together by John Folse, a well-known southern Louisiana chef who once did a cooking demonstration at a restaurant I owned in Memphis. I have seen several fresh, locally made, artisan cheeses at the Crescent City Farmer's Market, but Creole cream cheese was not among them. However, you can make it quite simply with just a few ingredients. See recipe on page 179.

| INGREDIENT | QUANTITY |
|---|---|
| **THE TOPPING** | |
| Sour cream | 1 lb. |
| Sugar, granulated | ½ c. |
| Vanilla extract | 2 tbsp. |

**METHOD**

**THE TOPPING**

1. Blend all ingredients.

2. Spread the topping evenly over the cheesecake and bake for about 7 minutes. Chill the cheese cake, covered, in refrigerator overnight.

You will need some cheese molds for this recipe. Any size or shape will do. You need the molds so the whey will drain.

| INGREDIENT | QUANTITY |
| --- | --- |
| Skim milk, at room temperature | 1 gal. |
| Cultured buttermilk | 1/2 c. |
| Rennet (6 to 8 drops, or one rennet tablet—you should be able to obtain rennet in a health food store.) | 1/2 tsp. |
| Cream cheese molds | 6 |
| Cheesecloth | As needed |

**LAGNIAPPE -** Those of you for whom cheese-making is a virginal activity may not be familiar with rennet. This is the enzyme needed to separate the curds and whey. The actual active enzyme is something called chymosin or rennin and was traditionally obtained from the fourth (true) stomach of calves. The rennet you will buy at the health food store, however, will be from bacterial or fungal sources.

## METHOD

1. In a large non-reactive bowl (stainless or glass) combine milk, buttermilk, and rennet and stir.

2. Cover the container with plastic wrap and allow to stand at room temperature—between 70° and 80°—for 24 hours. Do not disturb this mixture because the curds will be forming and that is what you want.

3. Ladle the curds into the cheese molds that you have lined with cheesecloth.

4. Place the cheese molds inside a pan that will catch the whey that will drain from the cheeses.

5. Place the molds in the refrigerator for a minimum of 8 hours—up to two days. The cheese will become firmer the longer you allow it to drain. Be proud. You just made about 10 cups of Creole cream cheese. You are ready to make the cheese cake on page 177.

# pâte à crêpes

The word *pate* (without an accent) in French most often refers to a batter of a consistency somewhat thinner than a "dough." This is the French "pancake" batter. The crêpe differs from the pancake in that it is lighter, thinner, and unleavened (except for the eggs). Rarely, if ever, is it served alone. It is nearly always filled with something or dredged in a sauce. There are recipes for folded, rolled, and even stacked crêpes. The dessert crêpe preceded the savory.

| INGREDIENT | QUANTITY |
|---|---|
| Flour, all-purpose | 1½ c. |
| Salt | ¼ tsp. |
| Butter, melted | 2 oz. |
| Milk, whole, cold | 1½ c. |
| Granulated sugar | 1 tbsp. |
| Brandy | 3 tbsp. |
| Eggs, whole | 3 |

## MAKING CRÊPES

Crêpes may be made in just about any size or pan. The two most common formats are the 6-inch and 10-inch crêpes. They cook very quickly indeed and, if you use one of the above formats, will weigh between 1 and 2 ounces each. The best pans for making crêpes are thin iron (well seasoned) or stainless lined aluminum pans. You may, of course, use any nonstick pan you have lying around. Do observe the "resting period" in the refrigerator, though, to allow the gluten to relax. The crêpe will be more delicate.

## METHOD

1. Place all ingredients in a blender or food processor. Blend until all ingredients are thoroughly intermingled.
2. Refrigerate for an hour or two.

## METHOD

1. Place the pan on medium-high heat.
2. Cover the bottom of the pan with clarified butter.
3. After 30 or 40 seconds, pour the butter out of the pan.
4. Beat the batter lightly with a wire whip to compensate for any settling that may have occurred in the refrigerator.
5. Place a 1- or 2-ounce ladle in the crêpe batter—depending on which size crêpe is desired.
6. Ladle batter into pan. Tilt and twist pan with your wrist until the entire bottom of the pan is covered with the batter.
7. Return pan to fire.
8. Cook crêpe until a very light, slight rim of brown appears around the edge of the crêpe. Do not overcook, as the edges will tend to crack when you fold, spindle, and mutilate the crêpe.
9. Turn crêpe, using a spatula and your fingers. Cook just 15 to 20 seconds on the other side.
10. Slide the crêpe out of the pan and onto a plate. You may stack and hold these for several hours.

# blackberry crêpes

I have mixed memories of blackberries. Oh, I have always loved the blackberries themselves, but if they are growing where you do not want them, eradication is next to impossible. I had them in back of one of my restaurants in California, growing into the patio area. But I also have fond memories of going wild blackberry picking with my mother and father. They are kind of messy to deal with, and the "seeds" will get stuck between your teeth. But who cares?

| INGREDIENT | QUANTITY |
|---|---|
| Crêpes | 12–16 |
| Fresh blackberries, washed and cleaned | 3 c. |
| Granulated sugar | ¾ c. |
| Cream cheese, softened | 6 oz. |
| Sour cream | ½ c. |
| Blackberry liqueur | 1 oz. |
| Confectioners' sugar | ¼ c. |
| Heavy cream, lightly whipped | 1 c. |

### METHOD

1. Slice 1½ cups of the berries in half. Chill remaining 1½ cups.

2. Combine the sliced berries with the granulated sugar and liqueur and chill.

3. Cream the cream cheese, sour cream, and confectioners' sugar together.

4. Carefully fold in the whole berries.

5. Place a couple of tablespoons of the cream cheese mixture in the center of each crêpe.

6. Fold or roll the crêpes and garnish with the blackberry "sauce" you have made.

7. Top with a dollop of the whipped cream.

# raisin and brandy bread pudding

This is my version of the "traditional" bread pudding you would find at some of the older New Orleans restaurants. It is not nearly as "elastic" as most. What distinguishes mine from the older version is that it is much softer and lighter and may be "scooped" for presentation.

| INGREDIENT | QUANTITY |
|---|---|
| Milk | 1½ qt. |
| Bread crumbs, French | 4 c. |
| Sugar | 1½ c. |
| Eggs, large | 4 |
| Egg yolks | 2 |
| Cinnamon | 1 tsp. |
| Vanilla extract | 2 tbsp. |
| Brandy | ¼ c. |
| Raisins | 1 c. |

## METHOD

1. Bring milk to a simmer. Soak the bread crumbs and ½ of the sugar in the milk.

2. Beat the remaining sugar and egg yolks together in a mixing bowl.

3. Incorporate the hot milk and bread crumbs into the sugar and egg mixture.

4. Add the cinnamon, vanilla, brandy, and raisins.

5. Beat the egg whites until stiff. Fold them into the bread crumb mixture.

6. Pour the mixture into a full-size hotel pan that you have buttered.

7. Pour the milk mixture over the bread crumbs and raisins.

8. Place the pan in a deeper hotel pan in which you have placed an inch or two of water.

9. Bake in a 350° oven 35 to 40 minutes.

# chocolate bread pudding

This more contemporary bread pudding will have a very creamy texture. I like to make and serve the two puddings together with the Cranberry Sabayon (page 184).

| INGREDIENT | QUANTITY | METHOD |
|---|---|---|
| Heavy cream | 2 c. | 1. Bring cream to a simmer. |
| Chocolate, semisweet, shaved or chopped | 16 oz. | 2. Process chocolate in food processor. |
| Sugar, granulated | 1⅓ c. | 3. When chocolate is grated, add cream, slowly, in a stream to the food processor. |
| Eggs, separated | 10 | 4. Add approximately ½ of the sugar to the processor. |
| Butter, unsalted, cut into small pieces | ½ lb. | 5. Add egg yolks, one at a time. |
| Vanilla extract | 2 tbsp. | 6. Add butter and vanilla and continue processing. |
| Bread crumbs, white | 4 c. | 7. Remove the mixture from the processor and, in a mixing bowl, thoroughly blend the chocolate mixture with the bread crumbs. |
| | | 8. In the mixer, whip the egg whites until soft peaks form. Continue whipping as you add the sugar until the mixture is stiff and glossy. |
| | | 9. Beat ⅓ of the egg whites into the chocolate mixture to lighten it. |
| | | 10. Fold remaining egg whites into the mixture. |
| | | 11. Turn the mixture out into a full-size 2½-inch-deep hotel pan that has been buttered and coated with sugar. Knock out excess. |
| | | 12. Place the hotel pan inside a deeper hotel pan in which you have placed an inch or two of water. Bake in a 350° oven on the middle shelf for approximately 45 minutes or until the pudding is just set. |

# cranberry sabayon

This custard sauce is called Sabayon in France and Zabaglione in Italy. It may be served warm in a coupe, but is also used as a sauce, served warm, cold, and even frozen. It may be made with wines or various fruit juices as a base. Madeira or Marsala are the traditional wines.

| INGREDIENT | QUANTITY | METHOD |
|---|---|---|
| Whole eggs | 4 | 1. Combine eggs, yolks, wine, or fruit juice and beat together in a bowl. |
| Egg yolks | 8 | |
| Cranberry juice | 1⅓ c. | 2. Add sugar and lemon juice. |
| Sugar, granulated | 1¼ c. | 3. Place in top of a double boiler and whip vigorously over simmering water until mixture thickens—5 to 10 minutes. |
| Lemon juice | 1 tsp. | |
| Vanilla | 1 tsp. | 4. Beat in brandy. |
| Brandy | 2 tsp. | 5. Serve immediately or beat until cool with a whip, then chill. |

# coconut cream pie

Courtesy of Chef Donald Link of Herbsaint. Serves 8.

## INGREDIENTS / QUANTITY

### PASTRY CREAM

| Ingredient | Quantity |
|---|---|
| Heavy cream | 3 c. |
| Vanilla bean, split | ½ |
| Sugar | 1 c. |
| Cornstarch | ¼ c. |
| Egg yolks | 5 |

### MACADAMIA NUT CRUST

| Ingredient | Quantity |
|---|---|
| Macadamia nuts, toasted | ½ lb. |
| Flour | 1 c. |
| Butter | 9 tbsp. |
| Sugar | ½ c. |
| Egg yolk | 1 |
| Salt | ½ tsp. |

### ASSEMBLY

| Ingredient | Quantity |
|---|---|
| Heavy cream | 4 c. |
| Sugar | ½ c. |
| Unsweetened coconut, lightly toasted | 2½ c. |

## METHOD

### PASTRY CREAM

1. In medium, heavy-bottomed saucepan, pour 2½ cups cream and scrape vanilla seeds into cream. Discard pod.

2. Bring to scalding over medium heat.

3. While cream is being heated, combine egg yolks with sugar and cornstarch. When cream is scalding, add remaining ½ cup cream to egg yolk mixture.

4. Pour a few tablespoons hot cream into egg yolks, stirring constantly. Pour egg mixture into pot and turn heat to medium-low. Stirring constantly, cook egg and cream mixture until very thick.

5. Remove from heat, transfer to shallow container, and cover with plastic so film touches cream, preventing skin formation. Refrigerate until cold and firm, 1 hour or more.

### CRUST

1. Combine nuts and flour in food processor. Pulse until nuts are finely ground—and no more.

2. In mixer with paddle attachment, cream butter with sugar. Add yolk, mix thoroughly, then add nut/flour mixture and salt. Mix until smooth.

3. Form dough into ball, wrap in plastic, and then refrigerate until firm, about 1 hour.

4. Divide dough into two pieces. Between two sheets of plastic wrap, roll ½ out to 10-inch-diameter disc. Repeat with other ½. Line two 9-inch tart pans with dough and chill in freezer until very firm, about 30 minutes.

*continued*

5. Preheat oven to 350°. Place pie weights in shells and bake until light golden, about 15 minutes. Remove pie weights, prick all over with fork, then bake until golden brown, about 10 to 15 minutes. Cool on wire rack.

## ASSEMBLY

1. Combine heavy cream, sugar, and 2 cups pastry cream in mixer with whip attachment. Whip at high speed until soft peaks form. Add coconut and continue whisking by hand until stiff peaks emerge. Spoon into cooled tart shells. Serve immediately or refrigerate until service.

# bananas foster

This may well be Brennan's most widely known dessert; it is the most requested item on their menu. In the 1950s, Owen Brennan was trying to come up with a way to feature bananas on his menu. His chef, Paul Blangé, devised this dish, and they named it after a regular customer, Richard Foster.

| INGREDIENT | QUANTITY | METHOD |
|---|---|---|
| Butter, clarified | 2 oz. | 1. Heat butter in fry pan, sauté pan, or chafing dish. |
| Brown sugar | ¼ c. | 2. Add brown sugar and thoroughly incorporate. |
| Ripe bananas | 6 | 3. Peel bananas and slice lengthwise. |
| Cinnamon | 1 tsp. | 4. Sauté bananas briefly. |
| Banana liqueur | 1 oz. | 5. Add the cinnamon and incorporate thoroughly. |
| Rum, white | 2 oz. | 6. Add banana liqueur and rum, heat through, and ignite. Shake or stir pan until all the alcohol has burned away. |
| | | 7. Serve this over vanilla ice cream. |

# vanilla ice cream

This is a very simple custard ice cream recipe. I make it in an Italian Gelatio machine. You may use whatever ice cream maker you have, though. Use this with the Cherries Jubilee (page 189), too.

| INGREDIENT | QUANTITY |
|---|---|
| Heavy cream | 3 c. |
| Milk | 1 c. |
| Sugar, granulated | ¾ c. |
| Vanilla extract | 2 tbsp. |
| Egg yolks | 4 |

**METHOD**

1. Heat cream, milk, and sugar in a saucepan stirring until sugar is dissolved.

2. Beat egg yolks together in a bowl.

3. Add about a cup of the cream mixture to the eggs, slowly, in a stream, beating all the while. Add mixture back to pan.

4. Whip constantly with a wire whip until mixture thickens. This will take about 6 to 7 minutes on medium heat. Do not boil!

5. Strain the mixture and place it in the ice cream machine.

6. I set my Gelatio machine on about 45 minutes.

*cherries jubilee*

Both Antoine's and Galatoire's still serve this very simple dessert. I first had this dessert at Antoine's. My Aunt Maye took me there for my 15th birthday. She told me to order cherries jubilee for dessert. I wanted something else. I have no recollection of what. She insisted. Typical teenager, I grudgingly relented. They turned the lights out in the main dining room and sang to me when they flamed it. Do try my version with the fresh cherries. Thanks, Aunt Maye.

| INGREDIENT | QUANTITY | METHOD |
|---|---|---|
| Sugar | ½ c. | 1. Combine sugar and cornstarch in a bowl. |
| Cornstarch | 1 tbsp. | 2. Whisk in water and orange juice. |
| Cold water | ¼ c. | 3. In a saucepan, heat and stir till thickened and smooth and translucent. |
| Orange juice | ¼ c. | |
| Sweet cherries, pitted | 3 c. | 4. Add cherries and orange zest. |
| Orange zest, freshly grated | ½ tsp. | 5. Add Kirsch and return to simmer. |
| Kirsch (cherry liqueur) | ¼ c. | 6. Cook for about 5 minutes. |
| Brandy | ¼ c. | 7. Warm the brandy. |
| Vanilla ice cream | 1 qt. | 8. Portion ice cream in bowls. |
| | | 9. Add brandy to sauce and ignite. |
| | | 10. Ladle flaming sauce and cherries over ice cream. |

# baked alaska

Antoine's has been making this for as long as I've been alive. You may include just about any ice cream you like. I make my own for this dish. I include the pound cake recipe (page 192) should you be inclined to give it a try, too.

| INGREDIENT | QUANTITY |
|---|---|
| Pound cake or Génoise | 1 |
| Ice cream, chocolate, vanilla, and strawberry | 2 qt. |
| Grand Marnier or Cognac | 1 oz. |
| Meringue | 1 recipe |

## MERINGUE

| INGREDIENT | QUANTITY |
|---|---|
| Egg whites | 12 |
| Cream of tartar | 1 tsp. |
| Powdered sugar, sifted | 1 to 1½ c. |
| Vanilla extract | 1 tsp. |

## METHOD

1. Slice the cake into pieces 1 to 1½ inches thick.

2. Carve and arrange the cake on an ovenproof platter—in whatever shape you choose. Round, square, rectangular, etc.

3. Sprinkle about one ounce of the Grand Marnier or brandy over the cake.

4. Shape the ice cream over the cake, completely covering it.

5. Place the meringue in a pastry bag fitted with a large star tube.

6. Decoratively pipe the meringue over the ice cream and cake.

7. Bake the Alaska in a 425° oven for approximately 8 minutes or until the "peaks" have browned. Flame with a little of the brandy.

### MERINGUE

1. Whip the egg whites until they froth. Add the cream of tartar and continue whipping. Gradually add the sugar, a little at a time.

2. Add vanilla and continue whipping until mixture is stiff.

*pound cake*

This aptly named recipe called, in early versions, for a pound each of butter, sugar, flour, and eggs (10 medium eggs would be about 1 pound).

| INGREDIENT | QUANTITY | METHOD |
|---|---|---|
| Butter, unsalted, softened | 1½ c. | 1. Sift flour, salt, and baking powder together. |
| Sugar, granulated | 3 c. | 2. Cream butter and sugar together. |
| Eggs, large | 8 | 3. Add eggs, one at a time, and incorporate thoroughly. |
| Milk | 1 c. | |
| Vanilla | 2 tsp. | 4. Add flavoring agent and vanilla. |
| Grand Marnier or other flavoring agent | To taste | 5. Alternately, add flour and milk, blending all the while. |
| All-purpose or pastry flour | 4 c. | 6. Line two loaf pans with parchment paper and add batter. |
| Salt | 1 tsp. | 7. Bake for about an hour at 350°. |
| Baking powder | 4 tsp. | |
| Butter | 1 tbsp. | |

## PECANS

Nuts to you! More specifically, pecans. The pecan figures prominently in the cooking of New Orleans for several reasons. We can nail down the modern pecan industry to a specific time and place. In 1846 an African-American gardener named Antoine successfully grafted a pecan tree that yielded large fruit with thinner shells. This was done at Oak Alley, the well-known plantation between Baton Rouge and New Orleans. In 1876 he planted what came to be known as the "Centennial" pecan. This planting was the genesis of the modern pecan industry. The word "pecan" comes from a Native American word, paccan, which, I am told, meant "hard to crack." Pecans were a staple in the diet of Native Americans of the Mississippi River Valley. If you are going to make the following pralines or pie I suggest you learn how to pronounce the word. Do not pronounce pecan as if it were a topless tin cylinder in which one might relieve oneself in an emergency situation. The nut is a "pehkahn." Emphasis on the last syllable.

# louisiana pecan pie

What makes this pie authentic Louisiana is the Steen's products. If you are unable to obtain them, use dark Karo syrup (it contains a type of molasses) or any corn syrup in the same proportions.

| INGREDIENT | QUANTITY |
|---|---|
| Unsalted butter | ¼ c. |
| All-purpose flour | 1 tbsp. |
| Cornstarch | 1 tbsp. |
| Salt | ¼ tsp. |
| Steen's cane syrup | 1½ c. |
| Steen's dark molasses | ¼ c. |
| Granulated sugar | ⅓ c. |
| Eggs, large, beaten | 2 |
| Louisiana pecans | 1¼ c. |
| Vanilla extract | ½ tsp. |
| Unbaked pie shell | 1 |

## METHOD

1. Melt the butter without boiling it.

2. Remove from heat, add and thoroughly incorporate flour and cornstarch.

3. Return the mixture to the heat and add salt, cane syrup and molasses.

4. Bring the mixture to a boil and cook for about 3 minutes. Cool.

5. Blend in beaten eggs, pecans, and vanilla extract.

6. Pour mixture into an unbaked pie shell. (You may garnish the top with pecan halves if you choose.)

7. Bake in a 450° oven for about 10 minutes. Reduce heat to 350° and bake for an additional 30 minutes. The pie will still be just a little jiggly when it is done.

8. Serve your pecan pie with the Vanilla Ice Cream (see recipe page 188).

# pie crust

If you do not already have a pie crust recipe you like, this one may be made quickly in a food processor.

| INGREDIENT | QUANTITY | METHOD |
|---|---|---|
| All-purpose flour | 2½ c. | 1. Place the flour, sugar, and salt in the processor and pulse just enough to mix. |
| Granulated sugar | 1 tbsp. | |
| Unsalted butter, very cold, cut into pea-sized pieces | 1 lb. | 2. Add butter and shortening and pulse until you have a coarse texture. Should only take a few seconds. |
| Shortening, cold, cut into pea-sized pieces | ¼ c. | 3. Add lemon juice or vinegar. Pulse again briefly. |
| Lemon juice or cider vinegar | 1 tsp. | 4. Remove from processor and divide into two balls. Roll one out for your pie and freeze the other. |
| Ice water | About 3 oz. | |

**LAGNIAPPE** - One pound of shelled pecan halves equals about 4 c. You should have a couple of cups of pecans left over. Try making the Pecan Pralines (see recipe page 195).

# brandied pecan pralines

If there were to be one confection associated with New Orleans this would have to be it. It has a storied history. *The Picayune Creole Cookbook* (1901) describes Pralinieres who hawked their sweet wares on Canal Street around Bourbon and Royal at the turn of the last century. Invented in the early 17th century by a French cook named Lassagne and named for his boss, the Compte du Plessis-Praslin, the original pralines were a concoction of almonds and caramelized sugar. The ever-clever Creoles substituted pecans for the almonds and they have been made and eaten since the middle of the 18th century in New Orleans.

| INGREDIENT | QUANTITY |
|---|---|
| Pecans | 2 c. |
| Heavy cream | ½ c. |
| Unsalted butter | ½ c. |
| Light brown sugar | 1¼ c. |
| Vanilla extract | 2 tsp. |
| Brandy | 2 tsp. |

## METHOD

1. Place the pecans on a half sheet pan and roast for about 4 to 5 minutes in a 325° oven.

2. In a thick-bottomed saucepan you have equipped with your candy thermometer, bring the cream, butter, and sugar up to about 240° (this is what we call the "soft-ball stage").

3. Remove from the heat and allow mixture to cool for about 30 seconds.

4. Add vanilla, brandy, and pecans. Stir until smooth.

5. Drop spoonfuls of the mixture onto a sheet pan lined with parchment paper. In 15 to 20 minutes you will have pralines.

**LAGNIAPPE** - You will need a candy thermometer for these. Having a candy thermometer is a very good idea if you want to make candy.

# THE CREOLE NOUVELLE NEW ORLEANS RESTAURANTS AND THEIR CHEFS: PLACES I EAT

I have consorted with and am eternally grateful to the five chefs who have contributed to this book. I consider all of them squarely within the historical framework of the very best of Creole cookery. Yet they have gone beyond the traditional and taken the cuisine to new heights. Some, understandably, want to dissociate themselves from the multitude of restaurants grubbing for the New Orleans tourist dollar and calling themselves "Creole" restaurants. In this I support them. I have, in fact, separated them with this book. Characteristic of their dedication to using the very best of ingredients in their restaurants, several of them shop with the organic vendors of the Crescent City Farmer's Market.

## CRESCENT CITY FARMER'S MARKET

The Economics Institute, a nonprofit organization founded in 1995 at Loyola University (my daddy's alma mater), is the driving force behind the market. Farmers, chefs, consumers, and business leaders make up its board. Its stated mission is "to initiate and promote ecologically sound economic development in the Greater New Orleans region." This translates into operating and supporting the Crescent City Farmer's Market, a truly movable feast. Three times per week—Tuesday, Thursday, and Saturday, year round, rain or shine—the marketers convene at three different New Orleans locations, with the Saturday market (700 Magazine Street) being the biggest and best attended.

Not only does Saturday have the best vendor turnout, but it also features demonstrations by the best chefs in New Orleans. Most of the chefs in this book have given demonstrations and frequently shop there. Anne Kearney of Peristyle prefers to make her connection early in the week at the Tuesday market. Organic produce abounds at the market along with fresh seafood, artisanal cheeses, and specialty products. It is typical of these chefs that they seek out the best in local produce, cheeses, and seafood. Although the Farmer's Market wasn't around when I was growing up, I have come to know it well since learning of it from Robin Garr, author of *Reinvesting in America: The Grassroots Movements That Are Feeding the Hungry, Housing the Homeless, and Putting Americans Back to Work* (Perseus Publishing, 1995). Robin was kind enough to include a program of mine in that volume. The Market is truly a worthwhile project and place to visit while in New Orleans. Kudos.

## PLACES WHERE I ATE

I grew up eating in many of the traditional New Orleans Creole restaurants. In the summers, my Aunt Maye, a schoolteacher, would take me to her favorites. We ate regularly at Galatoire's, Delmonico's and Antoine's, where I had my first cherries jubilee on my birthday. We went to the St. Charles Hotel, where she once had the barber there shave off my feeble teenage attempt at a beard, and the Hotel Roosevelt where my godfather was the maître d' in the Blue Room. My father was partial to Manale's and Tujague's, where he took us on many occasions.

The restaurants I have selected are all chef owned and chef driven, an important consideration because several other wonderful restaurants could have made this short list had space permitted. New Orleans is home to many conscientious, creative chefs who have their own restaurants, such as Brigsten's and August.

Every great chef ultimately wants to have his or her own restaurant. The process of getting to the point where one feels one has the energy, knowledge, and wherewithal to do it properly is a plateau to which many aspire but many never attain. The chefs here have done it and are doing it well. With a talented, on-premises chef in the kitchen, you can be assured that your dining experience will be the best it possibly can.

Another of my criteria was staying power—restaurants that will still be in existence by the time you get to New Orleans. As things currently stand, I think it impossible to get a bad meal in any of these restaurants. I've eaten in all of them more than once (some many times) and at least one time anonymously in each. Herbsaint gave me a great view of Chef Link manning the cooking line—it is the only one with a "partial" exhibition kitchen—where diners may be seen by the chef. I got a glimpse of the kitchen at Marisol through glass panels in the kitchen's swinging doors. The other three maintain their rightful arcane culinary privacy.

I also wanted to avoid restaurants found in large hotels, or I would certainly have included Windsor Court's New Orleans Grill.

Not one of the restaurants is "new," yet none is "old," either. The oldest is Bayona, and it is a little over a decade in existence. All these restaurants have superb wine lists and knowledgeable servers. In almost every instance, I have been impressed with the servers' detailed information on the daily specials.

Bear in mind that I am neither a food critic nor a food writer. I am a chef. I am not looking at restaurants and food in the same manner a critic would. I have a pretty good idea how dishes were made and what the technique was and what the seasonings were when I eat in a restaurant. I have an eye for presentation, but I think that first and foremost the food should taste good. All great chefs are great cooks. Food is what eating is about. While it is true that we eat first with our eyes, second with our nose, and lastly with our mouth, if it ain't right when it gets to the mouth, the entire proceedings preceding that moment don't mean squat. Above all, these chefs are great cooks.

## Bayona
### 430 Rue Dauphine

The doyenne of this phase of new Creole cookery—a chef who pioneered the new thinking in New Orleans fare—would have to be Chef Susan Spicer of Bayona. I first ate Susan's cooking when she was chef at the Bistro at Maison DeVille around 1989. She opened the bistro as chef in 1986. While her apprenticeship in the early 1980s was French—under Chef Roland Durand at the Hotel Sofitel in Paris—her cooking also reflects her travels through California and Europe. Just a glance at the menus will demonstrate her eclecticism. And although Susan does not call her cooking "Creole," her inspired use of local ingredients, coupled with her culinary training and background, makes her dishes truly New Orleanian.

Not only does she hold sway at Bayona, but she has spawned two other restaurants on this list— Lilette and Herbsaint. She was originally a partner with Donald Link in Herbsaint but has since gracefully bowed out of operations there to channel all her efforts into making Bayona the New Orleans destination restaurant.

Bayona's plain facade is typical of the old Creole cottages in the French Quarter. The Creole cottage housing Bayona is 200 years old. This first impression is put to the lie by a very cozy interior and courtyard behind. Bayona is comfortable with an excellent wine list that goes well with the menu. Dan Brown, Bayona's wine steward, is professional and attentive.

Although Susan has operated Bayona for a little over a decade now, the food remains fresh and innovative.

Bayona and Susan Spicer have been showered with awards and accolades, ranging from the highest ratings from the American Automobile Association (AAA) and *Gourmet* magazine to the Mondavi Culinary Excellence Award. Definitely make a reservation as far ahead as possible.

## Marisol
### 437 Esplanade

If you approach Marisol from the side, the first thing you will encounter is the courtyard. It is lush and comfortable with a brick patio and wrought-iron tables and chairs—and a little eccentric. Chef Peter Vazquez and his wife Janis designed and constructed it themselves. I was struck by the stone elephant dispensing water in the center of the fountain. I thought there must be an interesting story here. Peter called Janis from the garden supply center and said, "I'm out here at a garden store and they have two kinds of fountains. Should I get the little kid makin' pee-pee or should I get the elephant?" She said, "Get the elephant."

Marisol may be among the first restaurants to have come together because of the Internet. Chef Peter Vazquez met his wife-to-be, Janis—a New Orleanian—on the Internet and moved from Bethesda, Maryland, to New Orleans in 1996. He had been chef at Thyme Square in Bethesda. "At Marisol I have the unfettered ability to create the foods of my imagination." He brings a refreshingly eccentric feel to his cuisine, and this quality comes out in the ease of his manner and personality.

Chef Vazquez's father was from Puerto Rico, and his mother was Dutch, so his eclectic cookery comes naturally. He was brought up near Pittsburgh, where his family raised chickens and gathered wild mushrooms in a nearby forest. He served his first apprenticeship in Williamsburg, Virginia, at the Williamsburg Regency Inn.

During my most recent visit to Marisol, Chef Vazquez was kind enough to send me out his Salmon parfait. If it is still on the menu, I can recommend it. We had a nice chat that evening. I find his seemingly casual approach to cooking misleading to the extent that his food is very professionally prepared and presented.

## Peristyle
### 1041 Dumaine

Anne Kearney was kind enough to spend a drizzly New Orleans Saturday afternoon chatting with me about food. When I arrived, her husband and coproprietor, Tom Sand, met me at the door in shorts and a T-shirt. Tom went about his business and took reservations while Anne and I sat at a table in the bar—a tastefully lean and spare space that looks just like a classic French bistro. The restaurant itself is small, and Anne and Tom intend to keep it that way in order to maintain their very high standards in both the kitchen and the dining room.

Anne attended the Greater Cincinnati Culinary Academy before moving to New Orleans. She gives Chef John Neal, under whom she worked at the bistro at Maison DeVille, great credit for her inspiration, grounded in classic French techniques and general attitude toward food. When Chef Neal left the bistro to open Peristyle in 1991, Anne went along as sous chef. The following year, she went to work for Emeril Lagasse, for whom she developed recipes, wrote scripts, and spent some time working the food bar in Emeril's. Although her cooking style was already in place by the time she went to work for Emeril, she gives him credit for teaching her much about the food business.

Chef Neal's untimely demise in October of 1995 saw Anne returning to Peristyle—this time as chef/owner. She told me she was down to her last $300 by the time they got it rolling.

Anne has a serene and Nordic countenance. She spoke quite deliberately, sincerely, and passionately about food and her mentor, Chef Neal, during the time we were together. Anne would describe her cooking as Provence influenced. She is a supporter of the Crescent City Market, too, meeting with fresh produce growers there every Tuesday and often ordering ahead from them. Constantly seeking out artisan farmers, cheese makers, and purveyors of the highest-quality ingredients Anne is the incarnation of the modern Creole chef.

In time, many of those who have worked with Anne in her kitchen will go on to achieve culinary renown of their own. She is a very inspiring woman.

Anne and Tom sold the restaurant to Tom Wolfe in the summer of 2004.

## Herbsaint
### 701 St. Charles

It was a fairly early Monday evening when I ate at Herbsaint, and it was very busy. I sat at a table near the back where I could watch the kitchen at work and watch the entire dining room, too. Although my only view of Chef Link was from the chest up, I could observe him "running the line" and plating dishes. The cooks were visible in the background. I watched the activity in the dining room and kitchen over a good bowl of fairly traditional seafood gumbo with andouille—not entirely unlike the one on page 34. I liked seeing this homage to the traditional, as most of his dishes are quite nouvelle in character. As a lagniappe, he sent me his Beef Short Rib on Potato Cake with Dijon-Horseradish Dressing, and I was certainly glad he did.

Chef Donald Link grew up in Lake Charles, Louisiana; attended Louisiana State University; and moved to San Francisco in 1993. While attending the California Culinary Academy, Link worked at the Elite Café, Scala's Bistro, and the Flying Saucer. He came to New Orleans in 1995 and worked with Susan Spicer at Bayona for almost two years. Returning to the Bay Area in 1997, he was instrumental in the opening of Jardiniére and Mojo in Palo Alto.

When he returned to New Orleans, he planned to make his dream a reality. "I moved to New Orleans this time to open my own restaurant. After talking with Susan we thought it would be a good idea for her to be a part of the restaurant in the beginning to get it off the ground as I had made a good name for myself in San Francisco, but not in New Orleans. That's how we started. For the last two years I have run the restaurant 100 percent autonomously." Susan and Donald created Herbsaint together and remain good friends, and she retains a stake in the restaurant. Her influence lingers in the creativity of some of Chef Link's dishes.

## Lilette
### 3637 Magazine Street

While this is not the only restaurant in New Orleans residing in a former drugstore—Gautreau's also has this distinction—it may well be the best.

Chef Harris worked at Café Allegro in Pittsburgh and Spiaggia in Chicago during the course of his culinary odyssey. An émigré from Pennsylvania, John Harris began his New Orleans career working as sous chef under Susan Spicer at Bayona. She sent him to France for a Creole festival, and he got stuck there. While doing apprenticeships in two restaurants, Amphyclese and Le Pre Catalin, he stayed with the Marui family, whose culinary doyenne was named Lilette.

When he returned from France, he took over the executive chef reins at Gautreau's, followed by a stint under Gerard Maras of Gerard's.

Lilette is on Upper Magazine Street, a considerable distance from the Quarter. As a rule in New Orleans, any geographic designation that involves "upper" means "south" and "lower" means "north." So the "lower" French Quarter is the northern part of the Quarter and abuts Marigny. Got it?

If you are into antiques, you may want to make an outing of it and travel this street teeming with shops. Once called the "Irish Channel," this area was home to thousands of Irish immigrants.

One of the impressive things about this Creole Nouvelle movement in New Orleans is the fact that I see no jealousies or unfriendly rivalries among the chefs. They are actually friends. The night before John Harris and I sat down and chatted about his restaurant, he had gone to a basketball game with Anne Kearney. This camaraderie and attitude bode well for the future of the New Orleans dining experience. The Creole tradition is more alive than ever and finds itself in good—and talented—hands.

# index

# Peristyle

## Starters

### L'assiette du charcutier
Chef's plate created daily for your culinary enjoyment

Daily

### Crispy veal sweetbreads
Tender veal sweetbreads sautéed then wrapped in prosciutto di Parma, roasted and served
over a ragoût of roasted pearl onions, wild & exotic mushrooms, Brabant potatoes and
artichokes *barigoule* in rich Marsala demi-glace

9.5

### Pastis poached Gulf oysters
Plump Gulf oysters gently poached in a rich Pastis cream with wilted spinach and tender
leeks, garnished with American sturgeon caviar and crème fraiche

10

### Mussels *bourride*
Prince Edward Island mussels steamed in an aïoli enriched saffron-shellfish broth with
Provençal vegetables, tomatoes and tons of fresh herbs

10

### Grilled sea scallops
Large "dry-pack" sea scallops with butternut squash-ricotta gnocchi, wilted spinach, apple
wood smoked bacon and spiced pecans, served with beurre noisette vinaigrette

11

### Pan-seared foie gras
Pan-seared Hudson Valley foie gras served over griddled pecan baba with a
cranberry preserve infused demi-glace reduction

*When available*

18

### Pissaladière – caramelized onion tart
Flaky puff pastry tartlet topped with roasted garlic puree, caramelized onions, Niçoise olives,
fresh Texas goat cheese and white wine brined anchovies

8.5

## Salads

### Peristyle
Tender baby greens dressed with our classic balsamic vinaigrette
and today's seasonal garnishes

7.5

### Warm salad of roasted fingerlings, frisée & Crottin
Garlic roasted fingerling potato slices tossed lovingly with crisp frisée, tender shallots and
Dijon-thyme vinaigrette then topped with crisp pancetta rounds and a slice of
creamy Artisan Crottin cheese

9.5